**New Directions for
Community Colleges**

Arthur M. Cohen
EDITOR-IN-CHIEF

Richard L. Wagoner
ASSOCIATE EDITOR

Gabriel Jones
MANAGING EDITOR

Are Community Colleges Underprepared for Underprepared Students?

Pam Schuetz
Jim Barr
EDITORS

Number 144 • Winter 2008
Jossey-Bass
San Francisco

ARE COMMUNITY COLLEGES UNDERPREPARED FOR UNDERPREPARED STUDENTS?
Pam Schuetz, Jim Barr (eds.)
New Directions for Community Colleges, no. 144

Arthur M. Cohen, Editor-in-Chief
Richard L. Wagoner, Associate Editor

NEW DIRECTIONS FOR COMMUNITY COLLEGES (ISSN 0194-3081, electronic ISSN 1536-0733) is part of The Jossey-Bass Higher and Adult Education Series and is published quarterly by Wiley Subscription Services, Inc., A Wiley Company, at Jossey-Bass, 989 Market Street, San Francisco, California 94103-1741. Periodicals Postage Paid at San Francisco, California, and at additional mailing offices. POSTMASTER: Send address changes to New Directions for Community Colleges, Jossey-Bass, 989 Market Street, San Francisco, California 94103-1741.

SUBSCRIPTIONS cost $89.00 for individuals and $228.00 for institutions, agencies, and libraries in the United States. Prices subject to change. See order form at the back of book.

EDITORIAL CORRESPONDENCE should be sent to the Editor-in-Chief, Arthur M. Cohen, at the Graduate School of Education and Information Studies, University of California, Box 951521, Los Angeles, California 90095-1521. All manuscripts receive anonymous reviews by external referees.

New Directions for Community Colleges is indexed in CIJE: Current Index to Journals in Education (ERIC), Contents Pages in Education (T&F), Current Abstracts (EBSCO), Ed/Net (Simpson Communications), Education Index/Abstracts (H. W. Wilson), Educational Research Abstracts Online (T&F), ERIC Database (Education Resources Information Center), and Resources in Education (ERIC).

Microfilm copies of issues and articles are available in 16mm and 35mm, as well as microfiche in 105mm, through University Microfilms Inc., 300 North Zeeb Road, Ann Arbor, Michigan 48106-1346.

Contents

EDITORS' NOTES

Community colleges serve an essential access function, enrolling 39 percent of American undergraduates, 48 percent of all public postsecondary students, and 52 percent of public college freshmen, including disproportionate numbers of students who work, raise families, or arrive academically underprepared for college-level courses (American Association of Community Colleges, 2006; U.S. Department of Education, 2007). For many seeking to enroll in college, "the choice is not between the community college and a senior residential institution; it is between the community college and nothing" (Cohen and Brawer, 2003, p. 53). Therefore, the quality of access provided by community colleges is critical to private and public well being.

According to Berkner, He, and Cataldi (2003), 85 percent of freshmen enrolling in community colleges in 1995–1996 intended to earn a credential, 11 percent sought a vocational certificate, 49 percent sought an associate's degree, and 24 percent sought transfer to a four-year institution to complete a bachelor's degree. However, six years after first enrolling, nearly half had left higher education without earning a credential of any kind. Other research suggests that as many as another quarter of entering students apply, enroll, complete assessment testing, and attend classes, but leave *before* the first official enrollment census is conducted (Birdsall, 1994). These disappearing students are considered not to have enrolled at all, indicating that the actual rate of beginning student departure is even higher than commonly cited (Bers and Nyden, 2000–2001). These high rates of attrition have remained essentially constant despite decades of research.

Why do so many beginning students leave community colleges before achieving important educational objectives, often before it is even technically possible to fail? Are these students unmotivated or incapable of succeeding in a college environment? Are there ways in which community colleges are organized or operated that do not meet the needs of students who leave early?

The quick answer suggested by most college studies is that attrition, academic underachievement, and other negative student outcomes are a function of students' lack of academic preparation, lack of commitment to educational objectives, or excessive work and family responsibilities, factors considered largely beyond the control of the college. On the other hand, Tinto (1993) estimates that less than 25 percent of all students drop out because of academic failure and more than 75 percent drop out voluntarily because of difficulties related to incongruence and isolation from the daily life of the institution. Incongruence is a lack of fit arising from a

WILEY
InterScience®
DISCOVER SOMETHING GREAT

NEW DIRECTIONS FOR COMMUNITY COLLEGES, no. 144, Winter 2008 © 2008 Wiley Periodicals, Inc.
Published online in Wiley InterScience (www.interscience.wiley.com) • DOI: 10.1002/cc.340

mismatch between the skills and interests of students and the programs or environment of the institution. Theoretically, this lack of fit could be reduced if the student adapted to the institution or if the institution adapted to the student or both.

However, few empirical studies exist that assess influences of campus environment on student outcomes. As Astin (1993) observes:

> Environmental assessment presents by far the most difficult and complex challenge in the field of assessment. It is also the most neglected topic. In its broadest sense, the environment encompasses everything that happens to a student during the course of an educational program that might conceivably influence the outcomes under consideration. Thus environment includes not only the programs, personnel, curricula, teaching practices, and facilities that we consider to be part of any educational program but also the social and institutional climate in which the program operates [p. 81].

For example, contact with faculty outside of the classroom is positively associated with student engagement, retention, and success (Pascarella and Terenzini, 2005). Because community college students consistently report spending less time with faculty than their four-year college counterparts, many researchers and practitioners conclude that community college students are less interested or less able to improve their chances of success in this way. However, approximately two-thirds of community college faculty are employed part-time, are rarely paid for office hours, and may have to leave campus immediately after class to teach at another institution (Grubb and others, 1999). Furthermore, part-time faculty report less teaching experience and less familiarity with availability of campus services (such as tutoring and counseling) than their full-time counterparts (Schuetz, 2002). These kinds of hidden structural obstacles make it harder for community college students to connect with faculty outside of class or to experience the kinds of student–faculty interaction that has been linked to enhanced student learning (Pascarella and Terenzini, 2005).

Although we know relatively little about campus-student fit dynamics and their influences on student outcomes, we do know that retention rates and other outcomes can vary significantly even among community colleges with similar student characteristics and course offerings (Bailey, Jacobs, Jenkins, and Leinbach, 2003). Thus, campus environment can make a difference in student outcomes—and particularly for underprepared students. As Maxwell (1997) reminds us, a motivated and prepared student will generally succeed at college-level work despite the variations in instructor skills, grading standards, or the appropriateness of the material covered where as an underprepared student generally will not. Arguably then, assessing influences of campus influences on student outcomes are most salient at community colleges where students are disproportionately authentic beginners, "without the sorts of early preparation, prealignment in terms of cultural values, and sociocultural resources that more advantaged learners at those sites have" (Gee, 1999, p. 1). This volume seeks to fill a gap in the literature by exploring ways in which community college campus environments help or hinder student success.

In Chapter One, coeditors Jim Barr and Pam Schuetz describe a shift in perspective from student-deficit to one that includes institutional influences on student engagement and success. Pam Schuetz describes a theory-seeking methodology in Chapter Two that identifies and tests a flexible conceptual model of college student engagement suitable for adaptation by college researchers and practitioners seeking to improve institutional leverage over student outcomes. In Chapter Three, Sanford C. Shugart and Joyce Romano describe the front door of Valencia Community College in Florida, a new Atlas online learning community and portal. Atlas connects students to tools needed to succeed including LifeMap, Valencia's interactive student guide to figuring out "what to do when" to complete their career and education goals.

Dennis McGrath and Susan Tobia examine campus culture as a resource that can be developed to support student success in Chapter Four. In particular, the authors offer recommendations for the development of culturally sensitive institutions through professional development for faculty, staff, and senior managers. In Chapter Five, Faisal Jaswal and Teresa McClane Jaswal present an overview of a tiered mentoring program (TMP) operating at Bellevue Community College in Washington. The TMP leverages the supervised expertise of veteran students to meet the basic mentoring needs of beginning students via a tiered structure conceptually similar but larger in scope than supplemental instruction programs used to support student success in at-risk classes.

Using data from the National Education Longitudinal Study Restricted Use File, Lisbeth J. Goble, James E. Rosenbaum, and Jennifer L. Stephan examine institutional predictors of college degree completion in Chapter Six. In particular, the authors assess whether institutional graduation rate is a good predictor of completion for students with different levels of academic preparation. Melinda Mechur Karp and Katherine L. Hughes in Chapter Seven conduct interviews with first-time community college students, exploring how institutional structures encourage or inadvertently hinder information networks that foster students' sense of campus belonging and success.

This volume also seeks to identify new perspectives and practices that foster the success of underprepared community college students. In Chapter Eight, Barbara Illowsky describes the evolution and implementation of the California Basic Skills Initiative, an unprecedented statewide collaborative effort to better serve basic skills and English as a Second Language (ESL) needs of community college students. In Chapter Nine, John S. Levin reports on a large field study conducted in thirteen community colleges across nine states highlighting the behaviors of college and government officials in the context of institutional practices and social justice.

Chapter Ten by Pam Schuetz and Jim Barr discusses the need for transmutation of internal power struggles in favor of shared creation and execution of a vision of college goals that transcends bureaucratic boundaries. The interest expressed in this volume in influences of campus environment on success of underprepared students is not intended to imply that the phenomenon is purely structurally determined. Rather, in tune with Mills's observation (2000):

> We study the structural limits of human decision in an attempt to find points of effective intervention, in order to know what can and what must be structurally changed if the role of explicit decision in history-making is to be enlarged. . . . We study historical social structures, in brief, in order to find within them the way in which they are and can be controlled. For only in this way can we come to know the limits of human freedom [p. 174].

Accordingly, this volume seeks effective points of intervention, to support underprepared students seeking to develop to their full potential as human beings within the context of a community college campus.

Pam Schuetz
Jim Barr
Editors

References

American Association of Community Colleges. *State-by-State Profile of Community Colleges.* (6th ed.) Washington, D.C.: American Association of Community Colleges, 2006.

Astin, A. W. *Assessment for Excellence.* Phoenix, Ariz.: Oryx Press, 1993.

Bailey, T., Jacobs, J., Jenkins, D., and Leinbach, T. *Community Colleges and the Equity Agenda: What the Record Shows.* New York: Community College Research Center, Teachers College, Columbia University, 2003.

Berkner, L., He, S., and Cataldi, E. F. *Descriptive Summary of 1995–96 Beginning Postsecondary Students: Six Years Later.* Washington, D.C.: U.S. Department of Education, 2003.

Bers, T. H., and Nyden, G. "The Disappearing Student: Students Who Leave Before the Census Date." *Journal of College Student Retention: Research, Theory and Practice,* 2000–2001, 2(3), 205–217.

Birdsall, L. *Factors Affecting Retention of New Students in Their First Semester: Fall 1992 Cohort.* Pleasant Hill, Calif.: Diablo Valley College, 1994.

Cohen, A. M., and Brawer, F. B. *The American Community College.* (3rd ed.) San Francisco: Jossey-Bass, 2003.

Gee, J. P. "Learning Language as a Matter of Learning Social Languages Within Discourses." Paper presented to the annual meeting of the American Educational Research Association, Montreal, Canada, Mar. 1999.

Grubb, W. N., and others. *Honored but Invisible: An Inside Look at Teaching in Community Colleges.* New York: Routledge, 1999.

Maxwell, M. *Improving Student Learning Skills: A Comprehensive Guide to Successful Practices and Programs for Increasing the Performance of Under-Prepared Students.* San Francisco: Jossey-Bass, 1997.

Mills, C. W. *The Sociological Imagination.* New York: Oxford University Press, 1959/2000.

Pascarella, E. T., and Terenzini, P. T. *How College Affects Students: A Third Decade of Research.* San Francisco: Jossey-Bass, 2005.

Schuetz, P. "Instructional Practices of Part-Time and Full-Time Faculty." In C. L. Outcalt (ed.), *Community College Faculty Characteristics, Practices, and Challenges.* New Directions for Community Colleges, no. 118. San Francisco: Jossey-Bass, 2002.

Tinto, V. *Leaving College: Rethinking the Causes and Cures of Student Attrition.* (2nd ed.) Chicago: University of Chicago Press, 1993.

U.S. Department of Education. *Digest of Education Statistics.* Washington, D.C.: U.S. Department of Education, 2007.

PAM SCHUETZ is a postdoctoral fellow at Northwestern University in Evanston, Illinois.

JIM BARR is a senior research analyst at American River College in Sacramento, California.

1

Are community colleges as institutionally underprepared
for underprepared students as these students are for
college-level work? Learning to listen to underprepared
students is a strategy community colleges must embrace
and explore at the institution level if there are to be any
significant shifts in student outcomes.

Overview of Foundational Issues

Jim Barr, Pam Schuetz

These are challenging times for community colleges. Enrollment continues
to grow and diversify while per student funding remains the lowest in
higher education. Accrediting agencies, state and local governments, local
governing boards, and the public demand greater institutional accountability. At the same time, many students arrive with poor academic preparation,
excessive work and family responsibilities, or a lack of focus on educational
objectives—factors typically correlated with a higher incidence of student
underachievement and attrition that is considered largely beyond the
control of colleges. Defining underprepared students as the problem is coun-
terproductive in a system where a growing majority of freshmen is underprepared. A shift in perspective is needed.

No one would argue with the logic that effective solutions emerge only
when the critical or foundational problems are correctly identified. For
example, if community colleges have been developing solutions for underprepared students when the actual problem stems from the ways in which
the institutional environment fosters or hinders the success of underprepared students, it would explain why robust institutional solutions that
improve student outcomes have not emerged over the past forty years. It
also explains why community colleges will be hard-pressed to bridge gaps
between incoming student skill levels and rapidly evolving workplace and
civic demands: They are using an educational paradigm that is not effective
for the majority of its students.

This volume presents a difficult question for community college
researchers and practitioners to consider. Are community colleges as institutionally underprepared for underprepared students as these students are

NEW DIRECTIONS FOR COMMUNITY COLLEGES, no. 144, Winter 2008 © 2008 Wiley Periodicals, Inc.
Published online in Wiley InterScience (www.interscience.wiley.com) • DOI: 10.1002/cc.341

for college-level work? In this volume, *underprepared* refers to a constellation of factors that together indicate that a student is not yet emotionally, socially, or academically prepared for college-level work. With increasingly diverse student populations, unstable funding, and a broad mission statement, there is no question that underprepared students are a significant challenge for community colleges. Is it possible, however, that the student characteristics typically associated with negative outcomes are not the core of the problem that generates low rates of first-year retention, program completion, and transfer?

Conceptual Focus

Although some community colleges still view student underpreparedness as an academic deficiency, most are becoming aware that a variety of social and personal factors may be involved and related to student success. Along with academic deficiencies in English and mathematics, other factors may be important, such as socioeconomic status, past educational experience, first generation and reentry status, and race or ethnicity. Malnarich and others (2003) offers an excellent review of the range of student attributes and issues associated with underpreparedness for college-level work.

The notion that the educational system may be underprepared to accommodate underprepared students is not a new concept. Educators concerned with the growing populations of nontraditional students in higher education during the 1960s had strong concerns about whether the growing proportions of nontraditional students would benefit from current structures of higher education. For example, the overall theme developed by K. Patricia Cross (1971) in *Beyond the Open Door* revolved around whether education could change sufficiently to accommodate the needs of the growing population of new students who were underprepared for college-level work.

When faced with the challenge of accommodating underprepared students, it is common for educators to ask the question, "What do we need to become more successful with students?" The foundations of basic skills education largely emerged from this question, yet the lack of progress with underprepared students over the past forty years suggests that it was the wrong question to ask. How could education have known what it needed for underprepared students until it had clearly determined what the students needed? Much of Patricia Cross's brilliance in relation to her recommended educational reforms emerged from her observations of what students needed to be successful. Perhaps the biggest barrier for *educated educators* is that they tend to assume full responsibility for a dialogue regarding solutions, forgetting that the *less-educated* students and their needs can be a critical resource needed to guide these discussions.

Learning how to accommodate the reality of underprepared students is a strategy community colleges must embrace and explore at the institution level if there are to be any significant shifts in student outcomes. This is not unexplored territory for community colleges, as English as a second language (ESL) programs have begun to examine and understand the reality of the challenges and needs of their students. This, in turn, has provided these educators with an understanding of resources and curriculum structure they will need to serve these students more effectively. The following discussion outlines some of the structures and issues underlying basic skills programs, rates of first-year retention, transfer rates to four-year institutions, student services, academic support programs, and the assessment and placement process.

Basic Skills

Community colleges have a long history and tradition of addressing the academic needs of students identified as underprepared for college-level work. First-time freshmen who test below college-level reading, writing, or mathematics proficiency usually enroll in associated courses that have been variously labeled as remedial, developmental, or basic skills (Lundell and Higbee, 2002). The expectation is that students will correct deficiencies and then enroll in college-level courses appropriate for the two-year degree or transfer to four-year colleges. In this volume, the term *basic skills* is used to describe all sequences of credit and non-credit courses located below college-entry level curriculum in mathematics, English, and ESL.

Historically, basic skills students in community colleges have been viewed as a peripheral student population and essentially the responsibility of mathematics, English, and ESL departments. However, this view is rapidly changing to an understanding that underprepared students represent the majority or central population of incoming freshmen.

Over the last several decades, interest has grown in the implementation of a variety of student support programs designed to enhance student engagement and integration within the college community by addressing both personal and academic development. Reading centers, writing centers, counseling, tutoring, supplemental instruction, and study skills courses seek to address the needs of college students more effectively. Collectively, this approach reflects the growing interest in a developmental education strategy over the older remedial education efforts that focused primarily on academic deficiencies (Boylan, 1995). However, there is a distinct lack of a defined and articulated basic skills curriculum, often exhibiting only the vaguest resemblance across instructors for content and grading standards. It is probable that the institutional inconsistency found in and across basic skills programs amplifies obstacles faced by academically underprepared students. Is this an illustration of where community colleges are underprepared to serve underprepared students?

Although some research indicates that underprepared students with the support of developmental programs can be as successful as highly prepared students, other studies find little systemic evidence that these efforts have been successful (Boylan, Bonham, and Bliss, 1992). For example, in the first national study of community college remedial education, Roueche (1968) found that 90 percent of students placed into basic skills level courses withdrew or failed, even at colleges where basic skills education courses were mandatory. Community colleges have had forty years since the Roueche report to improve the performance of basic skills programs, yet—aside from evaluations of small programs that cannot be scaled up to serve the general population—there is little convincing evidence that much has changed.

First-Year Retention

Reported rates of first-year retention have hovered near 50 percent for decades (Barr, 2007; Hoachlander, Sikora, and Horn, 2003; Tinto, 1975; Tinto, Love, and Russo, 1994). In what is called a revolving door syndrome, unsuccessful students who leave before achieving educational goals are replaced by new entering students. Colleges often pursue recruitment and enrollment management strategies to offset the impact of student attrition more vigorously than trying to understand and resolve the dynamics driving student attrition in the first place.

Although a 50 percent dropout rate may seem high, it understates the actual problem because a significant number of students are likely to be placed on probation—technically still enrolled at the one-year mark, but making minimal progress before being dismissed or dropping out. A more realistic view of overall retention in community colleges comes from comparison of the size of the student population a college serves and the number of awards and transfers recorded each year. For example, if a community college serves fifty thousand unduplicated students every year, but awards three hundred certificates and fourteen hundred associate degrees with an additional fourteen hundred students transferring to four-year institutions, the reality of student attrition becomes starkly evident. In this example, only six of every one-hundred students earn a credential or transfer to a four-year institution. So what happens to the other 94 percent? Of course, in this example, a 6 percent goal completion (3,100/50,000) would not represent the entirety of the community college mission because many students enroll to upgrade job skills, participate in personal or professional development, or maintain certificates or licenses. Nevertheless, even if the fifty thousand students were halved to account for these students, the overall completion rates for awards and transfers would only be 12 percent for the remaining twenty-five thousand students. Although the research is replete with studies on first-year attrition linking demographics of the students who remain and continue to enroll, few have examined the institutional dynamics and student characteristics associated with those who do drop out.

A recent study of freshmen who leave during their first year of enrollment provides a descriptive understanding of associated student characteristics (Barr, 2007). Of 19,489 first-time freshmen starting in four consecutive fall terms from 1999 to 2002 at a single community college campus, 10,278, or almost 53 percent, did not return the following fall. Forty-three percent of these freshmen dropouts were recent high school graduates, over 61 percent were between eighteen and twenty-four years old, over 70 percent had to transfer or obtain an associate degree as their stated goal, and 80 percent enrolled in middle- to full-time course loads (six to twelve or more units). Surprisingly, there was no evidence of significant disproportionate representation by high-risk groups. What all dropouts appeared to have in common was a general underpreparedness for college work and poor academic performance in both basic skills (below transfer level) and college-level courses.

For example, a recent survey by California community colleges indicated that about 90 percent of incoming freshmen tested at or below transfer-level math, and 73 percent were below transfer-level English writing (Brown and Niemi, 2007). When other nonacademic factors associated with underpreparedness are also considered, it is not difficult to see that between 70 and 80 percent of all incoming freshmen are underprepared for college-level work at one level or another. Compounding this situation is the reality that significant proportions of students with the same basic skills level also enroll in other college-level courses during the same term they are attempting to acquire the foundational skills needed for all academic learning. Instructors teaching college-level courses are beginning to ask how they can be effective in the classroom when the majority of students lack effective reading and writing skills (Lyman, Browning, and Barr, 2007). Clearly, creating an educational learning environment that can address the needs of all students given the sheer size of the underprepared student population is a challenge. So, how effective are basic skills programs for underprepared students?

Community colleges have historically provided basic skills courses in mathematics, English, and more recently ESL to provide students with an opportunity to address academic deficiencies. However, the more important question is whether this strategy effectively addresses the needs of a rapidly growing underprepared student population. In *Between a Rock and a Hard Place*, Roueche and Rouche (1993) strongly asserted that higher education was still failing to meet the needs of its underprepared student population. In the California community college system, the conditions reported by Roueche in 1968 have not shifted noticeably. The probability for a student enrolling in a transfer-level course after starting in a remedial level math class is only 10 to 25 percent for students beginning in a remedial English reading or writing course (Research and Planning Group for California Community Colleges, 2005). The lack of success in basic skills education coupled with first-year attrition is also reflected in community college transfer rates.

NEW DIRECTIONS FOR COMMUNITY COLLEGES • DOI: 10.1002/cc

Transfer

Community college enrollments have grown considerably over the past forty years. As a result of this growth, there have been greater numbers of graduates and transfers. However, when examined as a proportion of the number of students served, rates of graduation and transfer have not changed much. Moreover, why should they? If much of the student growth over the last forty years has consisted of underprepared student populations with whom community colleges have been largely unsuccessful, why would there be any real shift in the proportional graduation or transfers rates?

Low community college transfer rates have emerged as a topic of great interest recently as part of increasing pressure for outcomes accountability. However, it seems that associated discussion and research often sidestep the idea of finding ways to help more students prepare for successful transfer (Shulock and Moore, 2007). For example, much of the current efforts surrounding transfer rate appears to be focused on redefining the denominator to include only those students with clear transfer intentions (Horn and Lew, 2007). Given that this strategy may be an important step in defining transfer rate, it does little to offset the reality that relatively few students do transfer. Mirroring the paucity of change seen over the past decades in first-year retention or student success in basic skills courses, it should come as little surprise that community college transfer rates are also stagnant.

Student Services and Academic Support Programs

There is conclusive evidence that the support provided in student service and academic support programs can be transforming for underprepared students; however, these programs are often resource-intensive. Given the limited resources available to colleges, the number of students participating in these support programs is small compared with the large number of underprepared students who could benefit (Barr, 2007; Boylan, 1995).

It is critical to understand that these programs demonstrate that underprepared students have the ability to succeed at college-level work, but in general have not had the opportunity to do so. One reason is that most community college practices were designed and still operate to accommodate well-prepared students. If the majority of students entering community colleges are underprepared, then the challenges these students present (and experience) are not isolated in basic skills programs but exist across all disciplines.

ESL and Curriculum Alignment

Recently in California, ESL educators concerned with inconsistency and performance of ESL programs created insightful guidelines for describing and defining the sequence from basic skills through transfer-level courses

(CATESOL, 2000). The associated report provided K–12 educators and college educators in ESL with a more universal understanding of the challenges and issues associated with second-language students, such as assessment and placement practices, support practices, faculty issues, student issues, course alignment, and articulation issues. It is important to note that ESL programs could not fall back on the time-honored strategy of faulting the K–12 system for not preparing students. Unencumbered by this rationale, they appeared able to focus their efforts on developing strategies to accommodate the reality of their students. The resulting model represents a new perspective—a paradigm shift—that could be widely emulated and implemented at an institutional level. From this perspective, it is difficult to understand why community colleges would want to continue with an educational paradigm that identifies students as the problem.

Assessment and Placement Process

Astin (1993) suggests that "an extremely important source of potential environmental information is institutional records on students. . . . But perhaps the richest source of data on the students' environmental experiences is the students themselves" (pp. 84–85). Maxwell (1997) further observes that a motivated and prepared student will generally succeed at college-level work despite the variations in instructor skills, grading standards, or the appropriateness of the material covered, while an underprepared student will not. Logically, then, to understand the conditions and dynamics that interfere with the success of underprepared students, we should ask underprepared students about their campus experiences. However, there is no question that exploring the underpreparedness of the institution from students' perspectives can be uncomfortable, if not threatening, for many educators. When the student becomes the expert, many educators may resist the reciprocal role—truly becoming a student again. Nevertheless, it is difficult to imagine anything changing if we are not willing to make this transition.

What happens when we identify problems with outcomes for underprepared students to serve our own institutional beliefs and needs rather than from legitimate assessments of students' needs? Mandatory assessment and placement have long been considered a best practice, yet it is increasingly evident that current assessment and placement strategies are factors associated with low success rates in basic skills courses (Boylan, 2002; Roueche and Roueche, 1999; Shulock and Moore, 2007). Currently, the California community college system is exploring the feasibility of implementing a common statewide assessment process for English, math, and ESL placement (see Chapter Seven). Theoretically, a systemwide assessment process could offer significant economic savings, facilitate the portability of test scores across colleges, provide for more uniform course placement across colleges, and make possible a more centralized and efficient research validation process. From the perspective of community colleges and educators, the benefits are seductive

NEW DIRECTIONS FOR COMMUNITY COLLEGES • DOI: 10.1002/cc

and promising. However, will there be substantial benefits for students as well?

From a Student's Perspective. An assessment or placement process offers the opportunity to understand the level of preparedness needed for college-level courses in mathematics, English, or ESL. Students rightfully expect that an assessment instrument will evaluate their skill levels in a valid fashion, which in turn will provide students with a recommendation for an appropriate course level. Logically, students must have the assurance that the course they enroll in is in fact aligned with and reflective of the assessment recommendation. Similarly, students planning to take a series of courses should also be assured that different instructors teaching the same course have reasonably similar grading standards and teach the same core curriculum. Thus, when courses are organized into a sequence, students should have the assurance that the courses articulate so that skill levels developed at one level appropriately prepare students for the next level, regardless of the instructor they select. It follows then that curriculum practices and assessment instruments must be aligned both horizontally across instructors teaching the same course and vertically through the entire course sequence if placement recommendations can be considered authentic and effective from students' perspectives. Although it is generally assumed that these conditions are in place, recent research indicates otherwise.

Lack of Assessment Validity. To ensure that assessment practices function as intended, all colleges in California are charged with providing validation to demonstrate that student placements are appropriate. In 1992, with widespread concern over the lack of predictive validity, California community college researchers who were responsible for validating the commercial assessment instruments began to ask, "Why is there a weak relationship between test scores used for placement and student success in the classroom?" A flurry of research reports soon identified instructor-grading variation as a serious problem associated with assessment test validation (Armstrong, 1995; Boese and Birdsall, 1994; Rasor and Barr, 1993). Assessment instruments are designed with the assumption that there is a reasonably stable target (curriculum alignment and grading standards) against which it evaluates a student's level of preparedness. If this target is not stable—for example, due to widely varying instructor-grading practices or the type and range of content taught in a course—it is not possible for any assessment strategy to inform students with much certainty of their level of preparedness.

When studies indicate that the best predictor of student success in an English or math basic skills sequence is the name of the instructor because of the wide variation in curriculum practices, we glimpse the significant institutional challenges that underprepared students face. Most important, we begin to see that we have been asking the wrong questions in our quest for effective solutions by incorrectly defining students or assessment as the problem, when the critical problem turns out to be curriculum practices. There is no question that curriculum issues and instructor standards can be a highly contentious and emotionally charged issue due to traditional interpretations of academic freedom and traditional instructional practices. Nevertheless, the reality is that effective assessment practices can only emerge as a consequence of effective vertical and horizontal alignment of curriculum practices.

Conclusion

If community colleges continue to provide an academic environment largely designed for prepared students with the view that the underprepared students are the problem, there should be little expectation of any significant improvement in outcomes for most students. This volume attempts to step outside entrenched habits of viewing the underprepared student as the central problem to describe the efforts of others who have begun to nibble away at the old paradigm with new questions and approaches that focus on addressing the reality of student needs. If community colleges can find the courage and willingness to appreciate that that they are as underprepared for their underprepared students as these students are for their curriculum, it could signal the beginning of a major paradigm shift and a new universe of possibilities opening for exploration by both community colleges and their students.

References

Armstrong, W. B. "Validating Placement Tests in the Community College: The Role of Test Scores, Biographical Data, and Grading Variation." Paper presented at the Annual Forum of the Association for Institutional Research, Boston, May 1995.

Astin, A. *Assessment for Excellence.* Phoenix, Ariz.: Oryx Press, 1993.

Barr, J. "Freshmen Dropouts." *Journal of Applied Research in the Community College,* 2007, *14*(2), 105–113.

Boese, L., and Birdsall, L. "Instructor Grading Variation and Its Implications for Assessment, Advising and Academic Standards." Paper presented at the Research and Planning Group for California Conference, Gran Libakken, Calif., 1994.

Boylan, H. R. "Making the Case for Developmental Education." *Research in Developmental Education,* 1995, *12*(2), 1–4.

Boylan, H. R., Bonham, B., and Bliss, L. "The Impact of Developmental Programs." *Research in Developmental Education,* 1992, *9*(5), 1–4.

Brown, R. S., and Niemi, D. N. *Investigating the Alignment of High School and Community College Assessment in California.* San Jose, Calif.: National Center for Public Policy and Higher Education, 2007.

CATESOL. *California Pathways: The Second Language Student in Public High Schools, Colleges, and Universities.* Sacramento, Calif.: California Community Colleges Chancellor's Office, 2000.

Cross, K. P. *Beyond the Open Door: New Students to Higher Education.* San Francisco: Jossey-Bass, 1971.

Hoachlander, T., Sikora, A. C., and Horn, L. *Community College Students: Goals, Academic Preparation, and Outcomes.* Washington, D.C.: U.S. Department of Education, 2003.

Horn, L., and Lew, S. *California Community College Transfer Rates: Who Is Counted Makes a Difference.* Berkeley, Calif.: MPR Associate, 2007.

Lundell, D. B., and Higbee, J. L. (eds.). *History of Developmental Education.* Minneapolis: University of Minnesota, Center for Research on Developmental Education and Urban Literacy, 2002.

Lyman, B., Browning, C., and Barr, J. E. "Faculty Perceptions of Student Preparedness." Paper presented at Northern California Educational Summit, Weed, Calif., June 2007.

Malnarich, G., and others. *The Pedagogy of Possibilities: Developmental Education, College-Level Studies, and Learning Communities.* Olympia, Wash.: Evergreen State College, Washington Center for Improving the Quality of Undergraduate Education, 2003.

Maxwell, M. *Improving Student Learning Skills: A Comprehensive Guide to Successful Practices and Programs for Increasing the Performance of Under-Prepared Students.* San Francisco: Jossey-Bass, 1997.

Rasor, R. A., and Barr, J. E. "Refinement in Assessment Validation: Technicalities of Dealing with Low Correlations and Instructor Grading Variation." Paper presented at the Research and Planning Group for California Annual Conference, Gran Libakken, Calif., 1993.

Research and Planning Group for California Community Colleges. *Environmental Scan: A Summary of Key Issues Facing California Community Colleges Pertinent to the Strategic Planning Process.* Sacramento, Calif.: Research and Planning Group for California Community Colleges, 2005.

Roueche, J. E. *Salvage, Redirection, or Custody?* Washington, D.C.: American Association of Junior Colleges, 1968.

Roueche, J. E., and Roueche, S. D. *Between a Rock and a Hard Place: The At-Risk Student in the Open Door College.* Washington, D.C.: Community College Press, 1993.

Roueche, R. E., and Roueche, S. D. *High Stakes, High Performance: Making Remedial Education Work.* Washington, D.C.: Community College Press, 1999.

Shulock, N., and Moore, C. *Rules of the Game: How State Policy Creates Barriers to Degree Completion and Impedes Student Success in the California Community Colleges.* Sacramento, Calif.: Institute for Higher Education Leadership and Policy, 2007.

Tinto, V. "Dropouts from Higher Education: A Theoretical Synthesis of Recent Research." *Review of Educational Research,* 1975, 45(1), 89–125.

Tinto, V., Love, A. G., and Russo, P. *Building Learning Communities for New College Students: A Summary of Research Findings of the Collaborative Learning Project.* Washington, D.C.: U.S. Department of Education, 1994.

JIM BARR is a senior research analyst at American River College in Sacramento, California.

PAM SCHUETZ is a postdoctoral fellow at Northwestern University in Evanston, Illinois.

2

This chapter describes development and testing of a new conceptual model of community college student engagement that can be used to guide and strengthen institutional leverage over student outcomes.

Developing a Theory-Driven Model of Community College Student Engagement

Pam Schuetz

Community colleges enroll over half of all beginning public postsecondary students including disproportionate numbers of adult, first generation, low income, and other underrepresented subpopulations. Setting aside students who did not express a credential goal, 47 percent of those who first enrolled in 1995–1996 failed to earn a certificate or degree or remain enrolled six years later (Berkner, He, and Cataldi, 2003). Why are so many community college students failing to accomplish their educational goals? What can community colleges do to improve student retention and outcomes?

Attrition is defined here as leaving higher education before achieving one's educational objectives; it is often correlated with students' poor academic preparation, excessive work and family responsibilities, and a lack of engagement or commitment to educational objectives. Because these factors are considered largely beyond the control of open-access institutions, attrition is typically considered something the student does rather than something the student and college interact to produce. This conclusion may be erroneous, however. Tinto (1993) asserts that less than 25 percent of all students drop out because of academic failure, whereas more than 75 percent of students do so because of difficulties related to a lack of fit between the skills and interests of students and "the organization of educational institutions, their formal structures, resources, and patterns of association" (p. 89).

NEW DIRECTIONS FOR COMMUNITY COLLEGES, no. 144, Winter 2008 © 2008 Wiley Periodicals, Inc.
Published online in Wiley InterScience (www.interscience.wiley.com) • DOI: 10.1002/cc.342

17

Theoretically, person-environment fit could be improved if the student adapted to the institution, if the institution adapted to the student, or both. Attrition has been found to vary significantly by community college even after controlling for student characteristics and course offerings, suggesting that some colleges adapt to their students better than others (Bailey, Jacobs, Jenkins, and Leinbach, 2003). However, few empirical studies have explored influences of campus environments on engagement or related student outcomes. As Astin (1993) observes:

> Environmental assessment presents by far the most difficult and complex challenge in the field of assessment. It is also the most neglected topic. In its broadest sense, the environment encompasses everything that happens to a student during the course of an educational program that might conceivably influence the outcomes under consideration. The environment thus "includes not only the programs, personnel, curricula, teaching practices, and facilities that we consider to be part of any educational program but also the social and institutional climate in which the program operates" [p. 81].

Analyzing influences of campus environments on student engagement is a complex undertaking that requires an "overarching explanation for how and why one would expect an independent variable to explain or predict the dependent variable"—in short, a sound theoretical framework (Creswell, 1994, pp. 82–83). However, as Ary, Jacobs, and Razavich (1990) observe, "Education in particular has suffered from an absence of theoretical orientations; the main emphasis has been upon empiricism. Educators have been criticized for their continued concern with getting the facts rather than finding out the why" (p. 19). The result is a body of college impact literature that is "highly segmented, even atomistic, and virtually atheoretical [focusing] narrowly on individual programmatic interventions or overlook[ing] the wide variety of influences shaping an outcome" (Reason, Terenzini, and Domingo, 2006, p. 1).

Pascarella and Terenzini (2005) assert, "Since individual effort or engagement is the critical determinant of the impact of college, then it is important to focus on the ways in which an institution can shape its academic, interpersonal, and extracurricular offerings to encourage student engagement" (p. 602). For the purposes of this study, *engagement* is defined as a state of interest, mindfulness, cognitive effort, and deep processing of new information that partially mediates the gap between what learners can do and what they actually do (Saloman and Globerson, 1987). This study uses iterative searches of the literature, guided by data from campus observations, interviews, and surveys, to locate and test a theory that can be used to strengthen institutional leverage over student engagement and outcomes.

NEW DIRECTIONS FOR COMMUNITY COLLEGES • DOI: 10.1002/cc

Figure 2.1. Study Overview

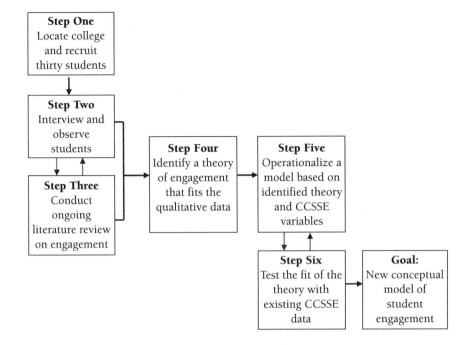

Method

Figure 2.1 summarizes the steps of data collection, analysis, and testing conducted over the 2005–2006 academic year at a California community college to identify a theory of student engagement.

In step one, a community college and student participants were identified for this study. In steps two through four, I collected participant observation and semi-structured interview data from thirty student participants to guide iterative reviews of interdisciplinary literature on motivation in search of a substantive theory resonating with the qualitative data. In steps five and six, I develop a new conceptual model of adult student engagement based upon the identified theory of motivation, using structural equation modeling (SEM) techniques to test the fit of the proposed conceptual model with data from almost one thousand large best practices community college (LBPCC) respondents to the Community College Survey of Student Engagement (CCSSE).

Length limitations prevent complete reporting of data collection, searching of interdisciplinary literature, or operationalizing and testing of the associated model of student engagement. (Details are available from the author on request.)

Preliminary Theoretical Framework. Although this study is intended to identify a theory describing campus influence on engagement, a preliminary theoretical framework is needed to make assumptions apparent as qualitative analysis is undertaken. As Shapiro (2005) observes:

> All observation is inherently theory-laden. . . . Among our central tasks is to identify, criticize, and suggest plausible alternatives to the theoretical assumptions, interpretations of political conditions, and above all specification of problems that underlie prevailing empirical accounts and research programs, and to do it in ways that can spark novel and promising problem-driven research agendas [pp. 15–17].

To draw the assumptions underlying my study into plain view, I conducted a review of the literature (not shared here due to space limitations) to frame a preliminary theoretical framework for this study. The framework draws from Bean and Metzner's (1985) student-institution fit model of attrition and several underdeveloped or underused models of environmental impact including Murray's (1938) theory of environmental press, Moos's (1979) social-ecological model, and Strange and Banning's (2001) campus ecology. Each of these models involve environment as a factor in conditioning students' perceptions of opportunities and subsequent attitudes and behaviors, which may therefore guide students toward attrition or toward success in achieving their educational objectives.

The LBPCC. The large best practices community college (LBPCC) selected for this study reported student retention and success figures that are better than the state average. The LBPCC is located in a suburban area approximately thirty miles from a large urban area and enrolled more than fifteen thousand students during fall 2003. The first-time freshman cohort is diverse: 40 percent Hispanic, 20 percent white, and 20 percent Asian. The proportion of the LBPCC student population twenty-four years of age or younger was somewhat higher than the state average. Freshman degree plans included transfer and no degree (40 percent), undecided (20 percent), degree and transfer (10 percent), degree without transfer (20 percent), and vocational degree or certificate (10 percent). Figures in this discussion were rounded to avoid identifying the institution and may not sum to 100 percent.

Participants. Adult students are usually defined as those over the age of twenty-four or twenty-five; however, the increasing diversity of the student population is eroding the discriminatory power of this definition. For example, eighteen-year-old students may be independent from their parents, with full-time jobs or a child, whereas twenty-six-year olds may be living as dependents with parents. This study focuses on functional adult students—defined as those who work at least twenty-five hours per week or raising a minor child while enrolled—a quickly diversifying, fast growing, and understudied subpopulation.

NEW DIRECTIONS FOR COMMUNITY COLLEGES • DOI: 10.1002/cc

I recruited thirty adult students, nineteen women and eleven men, to participate in this study. Twenty of the participants were between eighteen and twenty-four years of age, six were between the ages of twenty-five and thirty-four, and four were thirty-five or older. Eighteen were attending college for the first time at LBPCC in fall 2005. Fifteen had minor children, and seventeen were working twenty-five hours per week or more. Course loads varied from three and a half units to more than twelve, with a median of twelve units.

Qualitative Data. All thirty students completed a semistructured hour-long interview during fall 2005. Twenty-three were still enrolled when they consented to be interviewed a second time, at midyear. Thirteen who were still enrolled participated in the third hour-long interview during spring 2006. I also interviewed four students after they left the college, two of whom left early in the first term, one during the second term, and the last after almost three years of attendance.

Questions for the semistructured interviews were derived from a review of the literature on student retention and on adult learners and included references to the influence of the external environment (Bean, 1982), the influence of faculty-peer contact, and learning and motivation in the college classroom. Interview data were supplemented by observational data, gathered by following fourteen students through one of their typical days on campus and by campus visits that focused on three elements: ease of access to campus (public transport, parking, approach signage), campus way finding (ease of finding classrooms and services from signage, flyers, information services, and other sources), and campus service availability (location and hours of registration, admissions, financial aid, job center, and other student services, length of lines at key student service centers). The first site visit was conducted on the first day of instruction of fall term. I also went through the process of enrolling in a study skills class to capture a sense of the enrollment process first hand.

Quantitative Data. The Community College Survey of Student Engagement (CCSSE) "asks students about their college experiences—how they spend their time; what they feel they have gained from their classes; how they assess their relationships and interactions with faculty, counselors, and peers; what kinds of work they are challenged to do; how the college supports their learning; and so on" (CCSEE, 2008, n.p.). I obtained CCSSE engagement survey data for LBPCC to test the proposed conceptual model of engagement identified in this study.

The original data file provided by LBPCC contained information on almost 1,300 students. After I eliminated cases missing key variables, 1,148 cases remained for the final analysis—689 adult students (over the age of 18, working at least 25 hours per week or raising a child) and 459 non-adult students. I separated data into three samples: Adult1 ($n = 344$; used to develop and test the initial model); Adult2 ($n = 345$; used to retest the model), and Nonadult ($n = 459$; used to test the fit of the model for nonadult students).

Quantitative Analysis of Fit. Structural equation modeling (SEM) is a theory-driven comprehensive statistical approach for testing theory-based hypotheses about relationships among observed (measured) and latent (hypothetical or theoretical) variables. SEM analysis is superior to multiple regression techniques for this study because it allows explicit model measurement error in observed (CCSSE) variables as well as representation of both direct and indirect effects of variables. I used Mplus 4.2, a user-friendly version of the software to run the analyses.

Limitations. Potential methodological problems with the qualitative approach beginning this study (poor representation, overgeneralization, unexamined researcher bias) are offset but perhaps not eliminated by triangulation between member checks (face validity), checks with fellow education graduate students and faculty, tape recording and transcribing interviews, researcher journaling, and archival research throughout the project (Lather, 1986).

It is important to note that SEM analysis can only disconfirm a particular model. In other words, even if an analysis shows a good fit with the data, there may be other models that fit as well or better than the chosen model. In addition, the quantitative modeling of theory in this study is restricted to items contained in the CCSSE survey and it is possible that important variables have been left out. Furthermore, SEM embeds assumptions of linearity into the analysis even though the phenomenon of engagement may not be a linear function. In addition, the CCSSE database that is used to drive the SEM analysis is cross-sectional in nature and so does not allow modeling of engagement as a temporal or dynamic function—which it almost certainly is.

External validity involves the extent to which the conclusions from a statistical evaluation of a sample of students can be extended beyond the sample to the general population. Undetected variations within and across different campus environments and populations may threaten external validity of results. It is also possible that an inadvertent lack of rigor in the methods (poor sampling, incorrect observations, or interim conclusions about the dynamics of engagement) can introduce errors into the selection of a substantive theory or into subsequent modeling of associated relationships.

Findings

Triangulation of data and themes derived from observations and interviews guided interdisciplinary searches through the literature, inductively identifying self-determination theory (SDT) as a good conceptual fit to this study's data (Deci and Ryan, 1985, 2000, 2002).

Similar to positive psychology and resilience theories, SDT argues that engagement should be considered a common rather than extraordinary human characteristic, one that emerges naturally unless impeded or suppressed by social-contextual factors (Deci and Ryan, 1985, 2000; Masten, 2001). Specifically, SDT suggests that if sociocultural systems are robustly supporting student experiences of relatedness or belonging, competence, and autonomy, then engagement will occur spontaneously—even for students who have survived great adversity. On the other hand, if these three basic needs are not met, then engagement is less than complete, missing some essential elements to describe the deeply felt *what* (content) and *why* (process) of goal pursuits (Deci and Ryan, 2000).

Belonging. According to SDT, a sense of belonging tends to make innate growth tendency more robust and may be particularly important in fostering engagement in orientations and other early campus experiences. Belonging tends to arise from supportive and caring relationships where one's thoughts and feelings are valued. For example, Josephina, a forty-five-year-old mother of eight children who left high school at the age of fifteen, describes the sense of belonging she feels at LBPCC:

> I am very happy to come to this college. I've been to a lot of other [community colleges] but I found that this one is the best for me. I found a lot of help here. If you qualify, they give you a lot of programs and you don't need to buy any books. They give you free classes and everything. . . . The people say, "You can do it. Let's go. Fill this paper. . . ." Yeah, I feel like I'm a little part of this college. I think this college belongs to me and is a little family.

Competence. Deci and Ryan (2000) consider competence the most straightforward of psychological needs, related to the pleasure in being effective in social contexts. Competence is experienced through exploring and trying to master one's environment, essentially to performing well. Independent work in class, opportunities to talk, timely hints, and perspective-taking statements from instructors rather than narrow prescriptive solutions foster the experience of competence. For example, Deserie, a twenty-six-year-old mother of two, says:

> Our level of academics is much higher here [at LBPCC] . . . like our math, I hate math and a lot of students have problems, failing it here, and then they go to [other local colleges] and ace it. Here it's a higher level . . . like homework only counts for so much of the grade. Over there it's like hardly any tests or work in class. . . . Yeah, you feel a little more smart you know . . . even everyday, too, you catch things that you didn't catch before.

Autonomy. Related to volition, autonomy is the individually defined desire to self-organize experience and behavior to resonate with one's integrated sense of self. Autonomy (self-determination) is experienced through "choicefulness and authorship of behavior." A sense of autonomy is connected to students' clarity about what they value most in educational objectives or career opportunities offered and their ability to determine and follow through on steps required to attain the related objectives.

Autonomy is not the same as internal locus of control, independence, or individualism (Ryan, 1995). SDT defines autonomy not by detachment from others, but by the feeling of volition that can accompany any act, whether dependent or independent, collectivist or individualist. Students experience autonomy when freely seeking information on careers, programs, or options congruent with their own interests and personalities. Students experience increasing autonomy as they identify what they value most in educational objectives, determine steps to follow to complete a program, and work hard to attain a career option. Environments that provide choice, acknowledge students' inner experiences, and offer freedom to pursue their own agendas in a supportive structure foster autonomy. For example, Manny, a nineteen-year-old Latino student, says

> Now I've tried [two other local community colleges] but I just didn't like the structure, the classes, and the order in which you have to take them to be able to transfer, and from the research I did, I found that [LBPCC] offered the most rigorous science and English courses which is something that really interests me. . . . Here, the faculty expects much more out of the student. . . . The faculty here is awesome, extremely dedicated, and that just is what is going to keep me here. It really makes a difference, yeah. I want to further advance myself. I can care less about grades. As long as I feel I've learned something and feel that I've improved myself, that's all that matters.

According to SDT, community college student engagement arises spontaneously out of campus experiences that satisfy basic psychological needs that all humans have for belonging, competence, and autonomy. The next step in this study involves operationalization and testing of this SDT conceptual model using structural equation modeling and CCSSE variables and data. Length limitations for this chapter do not allow a detailed discussion of the conceptual model; however, Table 2.1 summarizes which CCSSE items were identified with the latent variables of engagement, belonging, autonomy, and competence.

Model Fit. The fit of the Adult1 sample of CCSSE data with the model referenced in Table 2.1 was acceptable (CFI = .964; RMSEA = .053 [90 percent CI = 037–069]; SRMR = .051), whereas the two other data samples (Adult2, $n = 345$ and Non-Adult, $n = 459$) were better, showing good fit with the model.

Depending on the sample used, structural equation modeling (SEM) analyses results indicated that the overall model accounts for between 50 and 60 percent of the variance in the latent variable of engagement. Interestingly, when the relationships among engagement and all other latent variables were represented as direct, autonomy was three times as strong an indicator as belonging while competence was not significant. After some thought about the nature of CCSSE items identified with latent variables, I ran another analysis representing an indirect relationship between competence and autonomy.

New Directions for Community Colleges • DOI: 10.1002/cc

Table 2.1. Community College Survey of Student Engagement

CCSSE Items[a]	Latent Variables* (Unobserved)[b]		CCSSE Items[a]
College helps student cope with work and family responsibilities (6d)		Belonging $\alpha = 0.72$	Relationships with faculty (8b) Relationships with students (8a) Relationships with administrative and office personnel (8c)
College encourages contact among students from different economic, social, and racial or ethnic backgrounds (6c)	Engagement $\alpha = 0.77$	Autonomy $\alpha = 0.77$	College experiences help develop a personal code of ethics (9l) College experiences contribute to gaining information and developing career goals (9n + 9o)/2 College experiences contribute to self-understanding (9j)
College helps student thrive socially (6e)		Competence $\alpha = 0.66$	College experiences contribute to thinking critically and analytically (9e) College experiences contribute to ability to solve numerical problems (9f) College experiences contribute to writing clearly and effectively (9c)

*(CCSSE) Items Identified with Latent Variables

[a]Item number in parentheses.

[b]Pearson coefficients shown are for the Adult1 sample (n = 344).

Modeling competence as mediated by autonomy (or self-direction) makes sense and strengthened the entire model. Thus, designing campus environments to foster development of self-understanding and commitment to related career options may also promote student competence and strengthen overall engagement.

According to SEM analyses, a sense of belonging (modeled as quality of relationships between the student and peers, faculty and administrative and office personnel) contributes less to engagement than competence or autonomy. However, belonging is also likely to be important in holding students on campus long enough to develop stronger connections of competence and autonomy. Therefore, freshman orientation, which most students described in interviews as a worse than useless introduction to campus bureaucracy, is a prime candidate for overhaul.

Orientation. Arguably, orientation activities welcome students to campus, introduce them to the kinds of educational opportunities available, resolve basic uncertainties about how to get started, suggest how to negotiate campus environments, and describe how to engage more fully in the college experience over time. Although some of this kind of information is procedural, other vital elements are not.

For example, interview data suggest that many LBPCC students have an entity theory of intelligence—either you are smart or you are not. Smart students succeed in college; others have difficulty or fail. This belief undermines student willingness to try something new or to ask questions because not knowing is tantamount to a personal failing of intelligence and it may seem better to quit than to fail. It is possible that open discussion of epistemological alternatives during orientation activities could awaken students' critical thinking abilities at an early stage while giving the institution an opportunity to present compelling evidence about how students succeed in college—without boring students to distraction or resorting to scare tactics. Seeing campus procedures and dynamics from the student point of view is key to supporting engagement from first contact to program completion.

Sample Variations. To explain differences in results for Adult1, Adult2, and Non-Adult samples according to SDT, one would first examine the immediate social contexts of the individuals involved and then their developmental or demographic differences to explore the degree to which their needs for belonging, competence, and autonomy were being better met. Thus, if we could track students through the campus environment—perhaps aided by transcript analysis or follow-up interviews—it is possible that we would find subenvironments (perhaps by instructor, course level, or department) or other campus variables (such as participation in small boutique student services programs) that could account for the differences in fit. The fit of nonadult data with this model may be an anomaly, but more likely it is verification that self-determination theory applies as well or better to nonadult students as to adult students. Although the latter would be in keeping with the universal humanistic qualities of the theory, more research is needed to assess this and other questions.

Conclusion

Self-determination theory (Deci and Ryan, 1985, 2000, 2002) resonates with LBPCC campus data, offering researchers and practitioners a way of thinking about the role of campus rules, practices, facilities, and climates in supporting or hindering student engagement. Even more than the "right" academic preparation or freedom from adult responsibilities of work and family, self-determination theory asserts that community college students who experience a robust sense of belonging, competency, and autonomy will naturally be more engaged. On the other hand, if these three basic needs are not met, engagement is less than complete, missing some essential elements to describe the deeply felt *what* (content) and *why* (process) of goal pursuits (Deci and Ryan, 2000).

The results of this study suggest that LBPCC could strengthen student engagement by fostering campus structures, processes, and relationships that help students feel an initial sense of belonging, buying time to develop stronger senses of autonomy, which, in turn, support competence and achievement. Of course, self-determination theory is not the only theory that might fit LBPCC or other campus dynamics. Furthermore, the interest expressed in this study in influences of campus environment on student engagement does not imply that the phenomenon is purely structurally determined. Rather, in tune with Mills's observation (2000):

> We study the structural limits of human decision in an attempt to find points of effective intervention, in order to know what can and what must be structurally changed if the role of explicit decision in history-making is to be enlarged. . . . We study historical social structures, in brief, in order to find within them the way in which they are and can be controlled. For only in this way can we come to know the limits of human freedom [p. 174].

Taken to its logical extreme, the methodology described in this chapter can help community college practitioners, planners, and policy makers to identify a theoretical framework that can be used to guide the design and implementation of effective environmental interventions in support of student engagement and success.

References

Ary, D., Jacobs, L. C., and Razavich, A. *Introduction to Research in Education*. (4th ed.) Fort Worth, Tex.: Holt, 1990.

Astin, A. *Assessment for Excellence*. Phoenix, Ariz.: Oryx Press, 1993.

Bailey, T., Jacobs, J., Jenkins, D., and Leinbach, T. *Community Colleges and the Equity Agenda: What the Record Shows*. New York: Columbia University, Teachers College, Community College Research Center, 2003.

Bean, J. P., and Metzner, B. S. "A Conceptual Model of Nontraditional Undergraduate Student Attrition." *Review of Educational Research*, 1985, 55(4), 485–540.

Berkner, L., He, S., and Cataldi, E. F. *Descriptive Summary of 1995–96 Beginning Postsecondary Students: Six Years Later*. Washington, D.C.: U.S. Department of Education, 2003.

Creswell, J. W. *Research Design: Qualitative and Quantitative Approaches*. Thousand Oaks, Calif.: Sage, 1994.

Deci, E. L., and Ryan, R. M. *Intrinsic Motivation and Self-Direction Behavior*. New York: Plenum, 1985.

Deci, E. L., and Ryan, R. M. "Intrinsic and Extrinsic Motivations: Classic Definitions and New Directions." *Contemporary Educational Psychology*, 2000, 25, 54–67.

Deci, E. L., and Ryan, R. M. *Handbook of Self-Determination Research*. Rochester, N.Y.: University of Rochester, 2002.

Lather, P. "Issues of Data Trustworthiness in Openly Ideological Research." Paper presented at the Annual Meeting of the American Educational Research Association, San Francisco, Apr. 1986.

Masten, A. S. "Ordinary Magic: Resilience Processes in Development." *American Psychologist*, 2001, 56(3), 227–238.

Mills, C. W. *The Sociological Imagination*. New York: Oxford University, 2000. (Originally published in 1959)

Moos, R. H. *Evaluating Educational Environments: Procedures, Measures, Findings, and Policy Implications*. San Francisco: Jossey-Bass, 1979.

M-Plus. (Version 4.2.) Los Angeles: Muthen & Muthen, 2006. Software.

Murray, H. A. *Explorations in Personality*. New York: Oxford University Press, 1938.

Pascarella, E. T., and Terenzini, P. T. *How College Affects Students: A Third Decade of Research*. San Francisco: Jossey-Bass, 2005.

Reason, R. D., Terenzini, P. T., and Domingo, R. J. "First Things First: Developing Academic Competence in the First Year of College." *Research in Higher Education*, 2006, 47(2), 149–175.

Ryan, R. M. "Psychological Needs and the Facilitation of Integrative Processes." *Journal of Personality*, 1995, 63, 397–427.

Salomon, G., and Globerson, T. "Skill May Not Be Enough: The Role of Mindfulness in Learning and Transfer." *International Journal of Educational Research*, 1987, 11, 623–637.

Shapiro, I. *The Flight from Reality in the Human Sciences*. Princeton, N.J.: Princeton University Press, 2005.

Strange, C. C., and Banning, J. H. *Educating by Design*. San Francisco: Jossey-Bass, 2001.

Tinto, V. *Leaving College: Rethinking the Causes and Cures of Student Attrition*. (2nd ed.) Chicago: University of Chicago Press, 1993.

PAM SCHUETZ is a postdoctoral fellow at Northwestern University in Evanston, Illinois.

3

This chapter describes how Valencia Community College in Florida developed a strategy that would move it from the already much better than average results in student learning, persistence, and success it was achieving toward the quantum level of improvement.

Focus on the Front Door of the College

Sanford C. "Sandy" Shugart, Joyce C. Romano

In the mid-1990s, Valencia Community College was in the early stages of what was then called the Learning Centered Initiative. As a part of this process, a consultant was engaged to work with the student affairs staff in planning their new initiatives to support improved student success and learning. During one of the meetings with a large number of staff, the consultant asked, "Does Valencia have an underlying model of student development to guide its strategies in deploying resources in student development and services?" Someone in the room spoke up and said, "Yes!" The consultant then asked, "What is it?" After a long pause, the same staff member called out, "No!"

This was a signal moment, a turning point in the college-wide conversation concerning the improvement of student learning. Absent any other conscious model of engagement, the college had gravitated to the dominant mode of service in our culture—retail customer service—and to perfecting its operations. Services had been thoughtfully clustered and physically arranged so students would experience a more rational service delivery model in something of a food court on each of the several campuses. Leadership for these services had been centralized, even though academic services remained somewhat decentralized, an important step toward assuring consistency of services and enabling the very conversation in which the consultant was engaged with the college. Communication systems with prospective and current students had been rationalized around a local adaptation of enrollment management. However, none of this effort had yet

New Directions for Community Colleges, no. 144, Winter 2008 © 2008 Wiley Periodicals, Inc.
Published online in Wiley InterScience (www.interscience.wiley.com) • DOI: 10.1002/cc.343

matured into a model of delivery that spoke clearly to student learning and success. Moreover, the fundamental organizational culture was still somewhat siloed, both within student affairs and across the other major divisions of the college, especially in academic affairs. The college fundamentally lacked a strategy that would move it from the already much better than average results in student learning, persistence, and success it was achieving toward the quantum level of improvement that was being discussed among its many learning-centered change agents. This lack of a "hedgehog concept" (a strong and concrete paradigm around which the strategy of improvement is built) was an important obstacle to the college achieving results that would take it from good to great (Collins, 2001). The lack of such a strategy was not caused by an absence of concern for or expertise in student learning and success. Rather, this disconnect was the result of a lack of a clear theory of work on which to build a strategy that could contribute powerfully to these important outcomes.

This chapter describes how such a theory of work was developed and how it resulted in new and powerful strategies for improving student performance by focusing much of our effort on the earliest experiences of students in their transition to college, both in the classroom and in the systems and processes of induction into the college, as we now say, "at the front door."

Valencia Community College

Founded in 1967 in Orlando, Florida, Valencia serves some fifty thousand credit students per year (unduplicated head count) on six campuses; two-thirds of the student body are pursuing Associate of Arts degrees towards college transfer and one-third are in technical degree and certificate programs. In the mid-1990s, the college began a deep and lasting dialog on the learning college paradigm (Barr and Tagg, 1995; O'Banion, 1994a). For the first several years, the work was preparatory, developing a common language and purposes for reform, and concentrating on staff and faculty development. By the year 2000, the work was beginning to shift to deeper changes in the systems, strategy, and intended outcomes for the college. A new strategic learning plan, adopted in 2002, signaled a focus on several important goals, including one called "Start Right," relating to much of the discussion below.

Developing a Theory of Work

There is an old joke about a millionaire businessman who is appointed to lead a distinguished academic institution. In his first senior staff meeting, he lays down the law to the vice presidents and provosts, indicating that he has always enjoyed success in business because he was ruthless in applying the discipline of business to his work, and he expected the same to be true of the university. "It worked for me in business," he declared, "and by golly it will work in higher education." The room was silent until the senior academic leader spoke up saying, "Well, we can see how that has worked for you in practice, but how does it work in theory?"

A real-life parallel to this in the work of educational improvement is the exhortation to employ the CASE (copy and steal everything) method. There is certainly nothing wrong with learning from one another's work and avoiding the reinvention of the wheel; nevertheless, there is a fundamental problem with reliance on this approach for securing lasting improvements in our work and that of our students. It is not enough to know that something works somewhere else; one must know why it works there, how our context differs from theirs, which theory the intervention is based upon, and more. This is especially true when there is no single treatment, no silver bullet that will secure dramatically improved results, as is usually the case in education. Because the environment for learning is shaped by dozens of people who are making thousands of daily decisions, implementing projects or treatments benchmarked at other colleges or gleaned from a best practices conference is likely to produce disappointing results. Simply copying other programs fails to engage influences and influencers beyond the treatment itself. What is needed is not just a new treatment, but a completely new pervasive approach deep in the college based on a shared theory of work.

Such a theory of work provides the connection between broad shared purposes and specific strategies at every level of the organization. It enables individuals and work groups throughout the college to contribute uniquely to the results with congruent effort, without the confining limitations of command and control. Having such a core model of work also allows genuine strategic focus where the college designs systemic interventions and evaluates their success, troubleshoots solutions, and interprets the assessment of their impact on students. The model, if developed out of genuinely collaborative effort, supplies the language of authentic reform and the basis for evaluation.

Valencia's theories for improving student performance emerged out of extensive conversations nourished by data and the best in professional literature and practice. Rather than leaping into problem solving, the college had the luxury and the discipline to keep itself in the mode of inquiry—open to data that described what students were really experiencing, wondering together what this might mean, and seeking explanations that could qualify as a theory worth acting on. These conversations helped develop a deep sense of shared practice among hundreds of participants, preparing the ground for naming powerful goals and seeking strategies that could achieve them.

What the Data Told Us

Even though we had developed sophisticated models of data analysis to gauge the effects of our collaborative work on student performance, it was actually very simple numbers that guided us to our most powerful theories of work. In this case, just three conclusions were seminal. First, we discovered that one of the most powerful predictors of graduation was success in the first few courses, just fifteen semester credit hours, on the first attempt. Yet our data revealed what we probably already knew only too well—far too many of our students experienced withdrawal or failure in their first courses at the college. This did not require a sophisticated data model; we simply asked, "What are the top twenty most difficult courses for our students, or operationally, which twenty courses have the lowest success rates as measured by receiving grades of C or better." Virtually all of these courses were typical of the first semester of many of our students. When we combined this with a ranking of our top twenty courses by enrollment, the pattern was clear: Many of our most heavily enrolled courses were also our least productive, with success rates hovering around 50 percent. Furthermore, these twenty courses accounted for nearly 40 percent of the total enrollment at the college. Because they were clustered at the front door of the college, they constituted a major barrier for many of our students.

This discovery, as obvious as it seems in retrospect, led to rich discussion involving hundreds of faculty and staff. The result was a sense of both despair and hope, a powerful potion for institutional change. We despaired that despite many efforts to improve developmental education at the college, so many of our students were experiencing failure at the front door. We were encouraged, however, by the thought that changing the pattern did not require changing a large percentage of the thousands of courses we offer. If we focused our efforts on just twenty or so courses, we could change the experience of thousands of students and launch them into an educational trajectory that promised dramatically improved performance throughout their careers, resulting in significant increases in the rates of graduation.

Our new theory of work, then, was very straightforward: improving student readiness for college and their performance at the front door would cascade through the rest of their programs at the college. Because so much of their first experiences of the college were mediated by their early contacts in the recruitment, transition, and induction into the college, a coordinated approach by student and academic affairs was essential. The shorthand language we created to convey this theory to one another in our work was captured in one of the seven goals of our Strategic Learning Plan: Start Right—Ensure that students experience extraordinary success in their earliest encounters with the college and establish a solid foundation for success in future learning.

Creating a Model of Student Support

Some of the earliest work based on the Start Right theory was in student affairs as they had already begun to think systemically and act on the theory. Teams of student affairs professionals, with faculty involvement, scoured the literature for a model that fit our students. The one that was adopted was based on a developmental view of first-time, in-college students and integrated insights from models described by O'Banion (1994b), Tinto (1993), Frost (1991), and Gordon and Sears (1997).

We then added several big ideas to the Start Right theory. First, we felt that our students must experience connection and direction. Engagement with the college begins long before the student's first classroom experience and is subject to serious improvement through thoughtful systems of engagement in student affairs and elsewhere. To engage students as learners before the first class and beyond became an organizing objective of systems design. Further, most students lack even a rudimentary education plan that will carry them to graduation. We found that most faculty and staff did not take their program planning seriously enough to ask students to write their plans down until their program was nearly completed and they filed an application to graduate. Here was an activity that could be productively moved to the beginning of a student's contact with the college. Our goal is for students to have a plan to graduate as early as possible in their program at the college, and we have developed systems to facilitate this.

On another level, it became clear that the processes, communications, tasks, and systems that students experience in student affairs ought to be considered a part of their overall learning environment. Accordingly, it is necessary to require intentional curriculum and real expectations for what a student is to learn. In addition, real expectations imply assessment of what is, in fact, learned. An important component of this is the notion of gradually transferring competence and responsibility to students as they learn. So early in their careers, the college assumes heavy responsibility for the student's progress through the institution. Nevertheless, gradually the student develops competence in planning and navigating his program and the college's systems, so he is capable to manage the next stage of his learning journey upon graduation. Planning, scheduling, and discerning future educational and career opportunities; knowing one's learning style; and applying this knowledge for one's own learning success have become a part of the curriculum of student affairs. All of these are incorporated into a new trilogy of systems that under-girds our model of student affairs.

LifeMap

The first part of the trilogy is LifeMap, a developmental advising model that promotes social and academic integration, education and career planning, and acquisition of study and life skills. It is primarily about student planning and goal setting; creating a normative expectation that students have life, career, and academic goals; setting up a system to establish and document those goals; developing assessment processes to evaluate and revise these goals; and documenting the achievement of goals. LifeMap describes for students what they should be doing for each of five stages of their development. Each stage of the model includes an outcome, performance indicators, and guiding principles that tie to the literature on best practices. The five stages are

- College Transition (middle and high school to college decision making)
- Introduction to College (0–15 credit hours)
- Progression to Degree (16–44 credit hours)
- Graduation Transition (45–60 credit hours)
- Lifelong Learning (learning beyond a first degree)

Details for the curriculum can be viewed online at http:valenciacc.edu/lifemap/stages.

The model was implemented and continues to be supported in three ways. First, there was a system redesign of virtually every process in student affairs based on a gap analysis of current practice and LifeMap ideals. Second, heavy investments in staff and faculty development about LifeMap enabled them to connect these processes, communications with students, and course experiences to the stages of LifeMap. Third, a consistent and creative internal marketing effort using engaging images and a memorable tag line ("Life's a trip, you'll need directions") worked to connect and direct students to LifeMap resources.

Atlas

The most visual expression of the LifeMap model to our students is the college's student learning portal, called Atlas. It is the digital expression of LifeMap. Developed with extensive collaboration from deans, faculty, and student services professionals with the purpose of enhancing student engagement and learning, LifeMap integrates numerous applications to support students in setting goals, exploring futures, planning to graduate, managing schedules, and documenting their own learning. Built on a standard student information system platform, most of these applications were homegrown at the time of deployment, although some have been replaced by tools now available in the marketplace. Other important features include direct e-mail to students, faculty, and staff; a home page for every course at Valencia, including an e-mail list of the class, a syllabus and outline, a chat room and message board; and Atlas groups that anyone on the system can create and join.

Most college portals include the standard tools for conducting business with the college, such as registration, progress reports, degree audits, payment records, and catalog information. To these, Atlas adds four important planning tools—My Career Planner, My Education Plan, My Portfolio, and My Job Prospects. Each of these has a wide variety of features to enhance student planning and is accessible to faculty, advisors, and other staff who assist students with setting and achieving their goals.

Atlas is introduced to all new students in the orientation program and is further supported by online tutorials for each application. The campuses support Atlas labs where students can use the system in a supported environment. In the student success course, which all new students are encouraged to enroll in, the curriculum includes Atlas, with time in the lab as a part of the course and the development of a plan to graduate in My Education Plan as a required outcome of the course.

The Service Delivery Model

The third element of the trilogy of systems is a new, learning-centered service delivery model. Like all colleges, this model at Valencia was designed to facilitate processes such as application, financial aid award and disbursement, assessment and placement, new student orientation, fee payment, and other essential transactions. However, we know that these processes are often frustrating to students—especially at the front door—and can create an early negative experience. In studying the literature on process reengineering (Bede and Burnett, 1999; Hammer and Champy, 1993; Hammer and Stanton, 1995), we concluded that a major problem in the traditional delivery model is that students get information in a disjointed, piecemeal fashion, reflecting the silos in our organization, about a process that is really end-to-end, from initial interest to a seat in a class.

The college redesigned its service delivery model so that students learn the entire model in one place with the assistance of cross-trained staff members who focus on the learning process rather than just giving answers to disjointed questions. Staff members are trained and encouraged to work with each student as a learner, guiding not only their immediate transaction, but teaching them one-to-one about the whole process and raising their competence in Atlas, where 80 percent of student questions and needs can be met. An important change in the model to facilitate this kind of attention was relieving the front-line staff from responsibility for telephone inquiries. Instead, all e-mail and telephone calls are handled by the enrollment services call center. Similarly, it was essential to separate the staff members who deliver direct services to students from those whose primary job is processing and verifying information. There are still offices that of necessity specialize in their services, such as disability services, but the vast majority of student services are now delivered in this more learning-centered, one-stop model.

Other Start Right Changes

In addition to the systems described above, a number of important procedural changes were implemented under the Start Right rubric. For example, the college

- Made a commitment to mandatory assessment, placement, and course sequence of students in developmental education, regardless of short-term enrollment effects.

NEW DIRECTIONS FOR COMMUNITY COLLEGES • DOI: 10.1002/cc

- Redesigned admissions, implementing a genuine application and admissions deadline as well as stretching out the process over several more weeks, to reduce daily traffic and allocate more time for advising, orientation, assessment and placement, and the other processes that need to be completed before the first classes meet.
- Added flex start terms, additional time periods during each major term in which students can start courses, so that students can get into classes after appropriately completing the induction process, regardless of when they start the process.
- Eliminated the negative effects of late registration and add-drop on the first week of instruction by adopting a policy that no students can be added to a class that has already met. This strategy in particular required serious redesign of our systems, in particular the development of a precision scheduling model to reduce or eliminate class cancellations and additions in the last few weeks of registration.

These strategies necessarily require deep coordination and collaboration among the student affairs and academic affairs leadership in their design, and all of the staff and faculty in their implementation. It is important to note that this strategy had the most impact on establishing a belief that the college leadership was genuinely serious about changing the conditions of teaching and learning in the college, earning credibility that has been essential to continuing momentum for thoughtful institutional change.

Start Right in Front Door Courses

As the work progressed, effort was focused on the experiences of students in both developmental first courses and in those college level courses common to the first semester or two, referred to in our work as *gateway courses*. Again, the simplest data best informed our theory and therefore our strategies. Of the ten most difficult courses in the college, seven were mathematics courses and two of the other three were applied mathematics courses such as macroeconomics. Therefore, we added the notion that the majority of our students struggle with quantitative reasoning and that securing improved results in mathematics would be fundamental to their success at the front door and beyond.

All of this work had been assisted by the college's participation in the League for Innovations' Vanguard Learning College and in the Lumina Foundation's Achieving the Dream movement. The former was particularly helpful in inculcating a culture of Learning First, another of our goals in the Strategic Learning Plan. The latter added to our agenda an essential commitment to closing the gap in student performance among students of different ethnicities, incomes, and preparation for college.

The college identified three primary strategies, already proven to work somewhere in the institution, to bring to scale across the entire college district, and to measure their impact by assessing gains in student success in six key courses. These were essentially three developmental mathematics courses, College Algebra, U.S. Government, and English Composition I. U.S. Government and English Composition were selected because they are high-enrollment courses with relatively low success rates for new students. Other Start Right courses would be added as the work progresses.

The first of the three strategies is supplemental learning, adapted to our needs from the nationally known model of supplemental instruction (Stone and Jacobs, 2008). In this model, students who have already been successful in a selected course receive training and take the course again as a model learner and peer to first-time students. Their role is not the same as a peer tutor, but like a tutor, they lend much needed support to other learners, both in and beyond the classroom. Coordinating this strategy with learning and math lab resources has proven very effective, resulting in substantial improvements in success rates for all students and an almost breathtaking closing of the performance gaps among students of different ethnicities.

The second key strategy has been the scaling up of the college's student success course. Taught as a three-credit-hour college-level course, a third of the first-time-in-college students had been taking this course in recent years. Our data have suggested a substantial positive impact on the performance of students at every point of the performance spectrum. Further scaling this program required moving from voluntary enrollment based on advising to mandating the course for students requiring the most substantial remediation. Again, the results have been compelling; the course has reduced student failure by a third among those mandated into the program, and the college is considering applying the mandate to a larger group of developmental students in future years.

Third among the gateway course strategies has been scaling up learning communities in students' earliest experiences of the college. These take several forms, ranging from linking Student Success with other front-door classes in a team-taught environment, to a variety of new course designs intended to create both academic and social connections for the students. Some of the most remarkable results have been achieved in these programs, with term-to-term persistence of our most at-risk students exceeding 80 percent.

Results

There are many ways to measure results at the front door. The results at Valencia have been remarkably encouraging, even though the college is still early in its application of strategies based on our theories of work. Two are especially notable. The first is student retention from term to term. Fall to spring persistence of students has grown during the period of these reforms from about 66 percent to more than 80 percent. This reduction in churning bodes well for the chances of students to achieve the milestone of success in the first fifteen hours of college. The second indicator of progress is success in the six gateway courses. In five of the six courses, success and persistence rates for all students have increased, with the greatest gains among African American and Hispanic students. In these courses, gaps in achievement have been all but eliminated a full two years ahead of our goals. The sixth course, the lowest level of developmental mathematics, has proven more difficult, and new strategies will be required to achieve results with these students. Nevertheless, our theories of work continue to offer hope that the right combination of interventions will yet be found.

Still to be confirmed is our theory that success in these early experiences will cascade into success in downstream courses, but the early indications are promising. The theories are what give us the common purpose that leverages actions, beliefs, and attitudes beyond our focused strategies that are essential to our success.

Conclusion

Most colleges adopt strategies to improve student performance. The experience at Valencia indicates that a focus on the front door, on creating strategies and environments that increase student engagement, holds great promise for significant improvements in student performance throughout the whole trajectory of their college careers. These approaches are successful because they are built on collaboratively developed theories of work that go deeper than mere best practices to shaping a culture of learning success for students. The common understanding that results from this collaboration unleashes the potential for all faculty and staff to contribute to student success, which amplifies the effect of the theory well beyond that of a few strategies. These same theories also serve to enhance the sustainability of efforts over the extended periods required to make a real difference.

References

Barr, R. B., and Tagg, J. "A New Paradigm for Undergraduate Education." *Change*, 1995, 27(6), 12–25.

Bede, M., and Burnett, D. *Planning for Student Service: Best Practices for the 21st Century.* Ann Arbor, Mich.: Society for College and University Planning, 1999.

Collins, J. *Good to Great: Why Some Companies Make the Leap . . . and Others Don't.* New York: HarperCollins, 2001.

Frost, S. *Academic Advising for Student Success.* San Francisco: Jossey-Bass, 1991.

Gordon, V., and Sears, S. *Academic Alternatives: Exploration and Decision-Making.* Upper Saddle River, N.J.: Gorsuch Scarisbrick, 1997.

Hammer, M., and Champy, J. *Reengineering the Corporation.* New York: HarperBusiness, 1993.

Hammer, M., and Stanton, S. *The Reengineering Revolution: A Handbook.* New York: HarperBusiness, 1995.

O'Banion, T. *Learning College for the 21st Century.* Washington, D.C.: Oryx Press, 1994a.

O'Banion, T. *"An Academic Advising Model."* NACADA Journal, 1994b, 14(2), 10–16.

Stone, M., and Jacobs, G. *Supplemental Instruction: Improving First-Year Student Success in High Risk Courses.* (3rd ed.) Columbia, S.C.: National Resource Center for the First Year Experience, 2008.

Tinto, V. *Leaving College: Rethinking the Causes and Cures of Student Attrition.* (2nd ed.) Chicago: University of Chicago, 1993.

SANFORD C. "SANDY" SHUGART is president of Valencia Community College in Florida.

JOYCE C. ROMANO is vice president for student affairs at Valencia Community College in Florida.

NEW DIRECTIONS FOR COMMUNITY COLLEGES • DOI: 10.1002/cc

This chapter illustrates how culture can serve as a resource to better support and assist at-risk students and offers recommendations for the development of culturally sensitive institutions through professional development for faculty, staff, and senior managers.

Organizational Culture as a Hidden Resource

Dennis McGrath, Susan Tobia

Although community colleges have long been the access point to higher education for low-income students and students of color, there is much work still to be done if our institutions are to fulfill their democratic promise. In this chapter, we draw upon a growing body of work described as the new equity agenda (Arbona and Nora, 2007; Bensimon, 2005; Hurtado and Carter, 1997; Rendón and Hope, 1996; Shaw and London, 2001), and supplement it with an analysis of the nature and role of organizational culture to suggest new strategies to improve the support and promote the success of underrepresented and at-risk students. In doing so, we view the community college as a border zone in which students must negotiate the transition between the values, beliefs, and practices of their home culture with that of the institution they are entering. Understanding the dimensions of the cultural challenges that students face when they enter community colleges will require revisions in our routine institutional research and increasing the success of at-risk students calls for new institutional practices and policies.

Estela Bensimon (2007) illustrates the issues that we address by discussing the concerns that practitioners of the new equity agenda have with much educational research. Bensimon argues that practitioner knowledge is systematically devalued in the scholarship on student success because of the influence of what she terms the dominant paradigm in higher education research. In the dominant paradigm, the student is the primary unit of analysis, methods are typically exclusively quantitative, and student success is defined as the outcome of individual effort. As Bensimon puts it, "The

image of the student [is] an autonomous and self-motivated actor who exerts effort in behaviors that exemplify commitment, engagement, self-regulation and goal orientation" (p. 447). In this paradigm, which dominates higher education research on student success, the student is seen "as the author of his or her success" (p. 447).

We can easily recognize the major features of the dominant research paradigm that Bensimon describes and trace its influence through countless studies of student achievement and persistence. Given the pervasiveness of the dominant paradigm, Bensimon's critique is particularly powerful, especially her emphasis that the theoretical and methodological assumptions of the dominant paradigm severely limit our understanding as they eliminate institutions as an appropriate topic of inquiry.

We draw on the work of Bensimon and other advocates of the new equity agenda here, especially their emphasis on the need to widen the frame of analysis to include the social and institutional contexts that influence the behavior of students and staff and the need to make sense of the experience of low-income and ethnic minority students. We believe these aims can best be met by "bringing culture back in," through a focus on organizational culture and the processes involved as students attempt to negotiate the transition between the values, beliefs, and norms of students' home communities and the cultural environments of community colleges.

We believe that this revised conceptual and methodological focus is a prerequisite to advancing the equity agenda. Because of the influence of the dominant research paradigm, there has been insufficient attention paid to the cultural dimensions of higher education institutions, either the values, beliefs, norms, and practices that shape their environments, or the cultural perceptions, values, judgments, and behaviors of our increasingly diverse students. To the extent that these topics have been explored in the higher education literature, they overwhelmingly reflect the use of quantitative methods that preclude the richer descriptions and understanding provided through qualitative research. Similarly, the programmatic responses to at-risk students that have been based on the dominant paradigm place primary emphasis on demographic features, academic skills, and individual effort and commitment.

However, to better serve our students, we must move beyond the blunt variables of demographic background and measurable skills to include the cultural dimensions of the challenges that nontraditional students face. These challenges include managing transitions between the cultural worlds of home community and college, renegotiating identities as they engage in academics, seeking opportunities to feel validated as competent students, and beginning to develop a sense of realizable new academic and professional futures.

A cultural perspective on these issues is critical because many low-income students and students of color are not well served by traditional institutional structures and practices. Research consistently finds that students most at risk are least likely to become involved in the social and academic infrastructures of institutions. The processes of academic and social engagement are different for students of color than they are for majority students (Hurtado and Carter, 1997). Consequently, merely offering opportunities for involvement is not adequate (Nora, 1987). To promote equity, we must revise our perspective on the nature of the challenge. The dynamics of student engagement and commitment require more than providing programs, hoping that at-risk and underserved students will take advantage of them. The central insight of the cultural perspective on academic environments is that *what we do with students and how they experience those efforts* have much more profound consequences than the resources that we offer or the structures we create. To understand the determinants of student success and failure fully, we must include organizational culture and social context. We need to both recognize the nature of the struggles that our students engage in as well as understand how the hidden resource of organizational culture can provide them greater support. A better appreciation of the symbolic and emotional dimensions of organizational culture can guide the development of programs and practices that engage students and transform them into active participants. As we will show, strong and well-managed organizational cultures promote student success by inducing hope for the future, enthusiasm about their studies, feelings of validation and support, and confidence in their ability to succeed.

In this chapter, we illustrate how culture can serve as a resource to better support and assist at-risk students. We briefly review some of the relevant literature for its cultural implications. We then offer recommendations for the development of culturally sensitive institutions through professional development for faculty and staff to enhance their ability to understand and respond effectively to students. We also offer recommendations for professional development for senior managers to enhance their ability to manage the cultural dimensions of their institutions.

Organizational Culture and Practices

Organizational culture is a powerful though subtle and largely invisible force in the lives of students, staff, and administrators. To manage organizational culture properly, it needs to be acknowledged and its features surfaced, mapped, and understood. Organizational culture is the invisible glue that holds an institution together by providing shared interpretations and understandings of events through socializing members into common patterns of perception, thought, and feeling (Kuh and Whitt, 1988; Schein, 1992).

Organizational culture is manifested in artifacts (visible products and activities), espoused beliefs and values, and underlying assumptions (Kuh and Whitt, 1988; Schein, 1992). Eckel and Kezar (2003) posit that an awareness of all three levels is important to an institution's understanding of its current practices and that all three levels must be aligned to effect meaningful change. For example, an institution that espouses active and collaborative learning as critical to student achievement, but accepts that the majority of faculty use lecture as the primary form of instruction, is revealing that information transfer is what is valued.

Eckel and Kezar's (2003) emphasis on the need for alignment points to the fact that effective, high-performing organizations have well-articulated, well-aligned organizational cultures, what Collins (2001, p. 193) calls a "core ideology," composed of widely shared values, beliefs, and assumptions that set priorities and guide actions and decisions. Shaw and London (2001) importantly note that culture is not just the core ideology, but also the organizational practices by which the beliefs and values come to be shared.

The Importance of a Strong Culture

As many organizational theorists have argued, a strong and well-articulated culture is a vital component of high-performing institutions because it provides a sense of identity, clarity of mission, and a focus to decisions, strategies, and practices (Collins, 2001; Kuh and Whitt, 1988; Schein, 1992). A strong organizational culture helps members develop a shared sense of who they are and provides clear values and beliefs to guide decision making and the formulation of long-term strategies. As Schein (1985) puts it, organizational cultures are potent and "feelable," which give them a "demand quality," provoking new members to respond, "do the right thing," and "fit in" (pp. 24, 28).

The emotionally charged nature of organizational cultures is captured in the psychological concept of appraisal of well-being. Appraisals are evaluations that actors make about the significance of a situation for their well-being (Lazarus, 1991). Appraisals, and the emotions they trigger, are rooted in the individual's attempts to interpret ambiguous situations for threats and coping resources. For instance, the degree of stress a person experiences is determined by the individual's perception of both the stressful situation and his or her ability to cope with events. As Lazarus notes, the match between perceptions of threats in the environment and one's coping resources generates positive or negative appraisals of well-being.

Theories of culture emphasize that the environment that is scanned for threats or supports is a social construction, an enacted rather than an objective reality (Berger and Luckman, 1967). The events that actors perceive and respond to as threatening or supportive are shaped by the culture. Organizational environments are constituted by the interplay of symbols and practice that organize experience for participants. McGrath and Van Buskirk (1993) say the appraisal process is culturally embedded. Strong organizational cultures help individuals formulate a "tool kit" of coping resources and generate strategies of action (Swidler, 1986).

These qualities of strong organizational cultures promote emotionally charged sense making in members, the process through which people make their situations accountable to themselves and others (Morgan, Frost, and Pondy, 1983). As Weick (1995) notes, sense making is vital in orienting participants and integrating new members because it provides shared meanings that help people work out what is happening to them and what they should expect in the future. An example of sense making is the positive effect that well-designed dual-enrollment programs have in promoting college access and success among low-income and underrepresented students. An outstanding example is the ACE (Achieving a College Education) program in Phoenix, Arizona. Sustained through collaboration among the Maricopa Community College District, the Phoenix, Tempe, and Glendale High School Districts, Arizona State University, and the Phoenix Think Tank, the ACE program gives at-risk students from low-performing inner-city high schools the experience of taking college credit courses on a community college campus while still enrolled in high school. As the first in their families to attend college, students often doubt their ability to succeed when they enter the program. In addition, the demands of the program—students take classes at the community college for six weeks in the summer and every Saturday for two years—seem like a major commitment. However, although many students report these misgivings, the supportive environment of the program resolves them quickly. Once they enter the program, ACE students are sustained by their new status as college students. In focus group interviews, the most frequent comment of the students was that "we are already in college." Before attending ACE, college often seemed to be an unattainable goal and a symbol of students' lack of academic success. However, these beliefs are soon debunked by being in the dual-enrollment program. Students are surrounded by others like themselves and by faculty who want them to succeed—all within a campus that soon becomes a familiar and comfortable environment. As several students commented, "By your first semester you already know the campus, you're not afraid, you feel confident. . . . You get to see what the teachers are like . . . you get to feel like a college student for two years" (McGrath and Van Buskirk, 1999, p. 13).

This example illustrates the limitations of the excessively rationalist assumptions of the dominant paradigm and the failure to consider the impact of organizational culture. Students, especially nontraditional students who lack family or peer role models, and who often come from low-performing K–12 schools, inevitably have doubts about their abilities and questions about their future when they enter academic environments. Students need to be cognitively oriented to the campus environment and helped to understand what they need to do to succeed, the demands that will be put on them, and to accurately assess the skills they have and the resources that are available to cope with the situation. At the same time, the emotional dimensions of the situation must be attended to as well. If students are to engage in the life of the college, doubts and fears must be quieted and students inculcated with hope for the future, enthusiasm for their studies, and a sense of validation that they are welcome and have a right to be there.

This brief review illustrates the importance of organizational culture as the hidden resource in promoting student success. If community colleges are to build on earlier successes and advance the equity agenda, they must attend to the significance of organizational culture and the practices that transmit it; they must revise their institutional research to better understand the challenges their students face and formulate new strategies to improve academic and social engagement. We do not claim to offer a full blueprint for action because there is much we still do not know about how students experience campus environments. Instead, we call on community college administrators, faculty, and staff to engage in the types of research and institutional reviews that will surface the core features of their cultures, identify the challenges for different groups of students, and experiment with new programs and practices. As Bensimon (2007) noted, advancing student success is a "learning problem of practitioners and institutions" (p. 446). She argues that we lack the necessary "funds of knowledge" and experience to recognize the "racialized nature of the collegiate experience for African-American and Latina/o students," and to "adjust our practices accordingly" (p. 446). We agree with Bensimon that part of the solution requires developing new models of practitioners as researchers and researchers as facilitators in organizational change efforts.

Advancing the equity agenda in community colleges cannot be fulfilled by simply implementing off-the-shelf programs. Developing effective strategies requires that we first resolve the learning problem of practitioners and institutions through a commitment to a variety of qualitative research strategies. We need to learn more about a number of dimensions of our campus environments. Some critical questions concern the different types of students and what they experience as the most disruptive dimensions of the transition to college, the types of first-year experiences that would be most helpful to them, the types of in-and-out-of-classroom experiences that give students the greatest sense of validation, and the types of classroom activities and pedagogical practices that promote academic engagement for different groups of students. Additional issues comprise the ways student service personnel can contribute to best create a sense of community and connection among students, the types of outreach and bridge programs that best raise student aspirations and encourage enrollment, and the ways part-time students can be better connected to the academic and social life of the college.

It is important to recognize that we already have a significant body of research and practice to draw upon in building the knowledge base that we need. Nora and Cabrera's (1996) student adjustment model and Nora's (2003) student-institution engagement model have advanced the theoretical and methodological framework needed to capture student experience properly. These models offer an advance over earlier work by emphasizing the unique interaction between the student and the institution. This interaction produces a connection between the student and the institution that leads to persistence. Research using these models finds that college-related factors, such as the encouragement and support received in interactions with faculty and fellow students, are as important as precollegiate factors in determining their retention and progress toward a degree (Arbona and Nora, 2007).

A variety of widely disseminated reports has converged in documenting the key elements associated with student success in postsecondary institutions. A review of *Involvement in Learning* (Study Group on the Conditions of Excellence in American Higher Education, 1984), *Seven Principles for Good Practice in Undergraduate Education* (Chickering and Gamson, 1987), and *Making Quality Count* (Education Commission of the States, 1995) identify institutional conditions important to student development and success. Such conditions include a clear, focused institutional mission; high standards for student performance; support for students to explore human differences and emerging dimensions of self; emphasis on early months and first year of study; respect for diverse talent; integration of prior learning and experience; ongoing practice of learned skills; active learning; assessment and feedback; collaboration among students; adequate time on task; and out-of-class contact with faculty (Kuh, Kinzie, Schuh, and Whitt, 2005).

However, as Kuh and others (2005) point out, culture is the critical dimension in each of these recommendations. A shared culture gives members of an organization a common language, a way to bring meaning and coherence to the multiple activities taking place across the institution. They recommend that institutions identify cultural properties that are barriers to student success.

Kuh and others (2005) found that institutions that demonstrated higher than expected levels of student success as measured by graduation rates and student engagement levels on the NSSE (National Survey of Student Engagement) shared an unshakeable focus on student learning. They maintained a view of students as people capable of learning anything their institutions teach, they collaborated across divisions, and they exhibited a positive restlessness—the inclination to continually improve, as they were never quite satisfied.

McLeod and Young (2005) hold that to be student centered requires that institutions recognize that academic development goes hand in hand with personal and social development. Institutions in which academic and student affairs divisions recognize the need for collaboration promote it through policy and practice. Furthermore, they argue that organizational commitment must be enhanced by a leader and a structure, which focuses the institution on the importance of student success, involves all areas up and down the hierarchy in proven interventions, and keeps everyone informed on student progress. Moreover, this commitment must be based in a strategic plan with committed resources, especially designated offices and individuals whose responsibility it is to keep the institution focused on student success and progress.

Rendón, García, and Person (2004) discuss ways of transforming first-year experience programs to make them more useful to students of color. Appropriate first-year programs need to recognize that students may be struggling with a new college identity that separates them from their families and peers and requires them to negotiate in multiple worlds.

A variety of studies of learning communities conducted at Seattle Central Community College, the University of Washington, La Guardia Community College (Tinto, Goodsell, and Russo, 1994), and Santa Ana Community College (McGrath and Van Buskirk, 1998) have found that learning communities help students engage in the academic and social dimensions of the college. Learning communities do so by increasing faculty-student interaction and providing opportunities for group study and interaction.

Recommendations: Developing a Culturally Effective Institution

Developing a culturally effective institution requires a reorientation of research, policies, and practices. Traditional quantitative studies must be balanced with qualitative research such as examining how the mission and vision is visible in the artifacts, beliefs, values, and practices of the institution and what these mean to students. It may involve identifying institutional symbols such as signage, student spaces, wait time for services, and asking how students perceive them. It may entail looking at services offered and the contexts in which they are offered and determining if they are welcoming and accessible, particularly for underserved students. A prevailing question is, what do we value and how do we show it in our procedures, our classroom practices, our budget priorities? For example, institutional cultures that make it easy for students to get involved (keeping libraries open evenings and weekends, offering support services to day, evening, weekend, and distance learning students, and providing engaging study spaces) send a message that they are serious about student learning. Qualitative studies must also document the perspective of various student populations. What are the critical experiences for these students? How do they make sense of the contexts in which they find themselves? Are they supportive or threatening and how do they cope if it is the latter? Perhaps more important than assessing the resources themselves is understanding students' perceptions of resources offered. We recognize that a reorientation of focus is a long-term effort and requires the commitment of many people throughout the institution. We see professional development for faculty, staff, and senior administrators as key in supporting this effort.

Professional Development for Faculty and Staff. Ideally, the key focus of professional development activities for faculty and staff is to enhance their ability to understand and respond effectively to students. There is a variety of ways to do this, and we recommend the following for consideration.

Listening to Students' Stories. Creating venues for students to tell their stories (where they come from, the values they bring, previous learning contexts, how they experience college) through orientation activities, informal presentations, or writing assignments can inform decisions about which pedagogical practices and strategies might be appropriate and effective. For example, group discussions may engage students who enjoy the social aspects of learning. Similarly, encouraging and paying attention to student questions may alleviate the anxiety of those students whose questions have been ignored in past learning contexts or who feel that it is not cool to ask questions in class. Likewise, understanding that students want frequent feedback to know how they are doing may lead to the inclusion of periodic formative assessments in a course. Listening to students' views on teaching and learning validates the experiences they bring. After all, students have spent more time in schools than anybody else except teachers (Nieto, 1994). Students are then more open, cognitively and emotionally, to integrate the values and traditions of a new academic environment (Rendón, 2004).

Reflective Inquiry. A promising venue for critically examining pedagogical practices is the group reflective inquiry seminar in which faculty share their assignments, exams, and student responses for the purpose of collectively determining their intended effects on student learning. For example, discussing a particular reading and the accompanying prereading questions posed can bring attention to faculty assumptions and expectations about students' prior knowledge. Examining a writing assignment along with selected student responses may generate insight as to why some assignments worked or did not work and lead faculty to make adjustments. Group reflections can take on a broader perspective by engaging participants in questions concerning their role in facilitating the transition of students to college. Such questions may address to what extent the classroom is set up to benefit primarily majority students; to what extent faculty understand what college transition means from the student's perspective; the positive and negative factors associated with attending college for students of color; and how faculty view themselves in relationship to students (Rendón, 2004, p. 182).

Culturally Responsive Teaching and Learning Strategies. McPhail and Costner (2004) note that 90 to 95 percent of participants proudly claim that they do not notice the race of their students when they enter their classrooms. Faculty development that places culture at the center of learning opens a dialogue about the educational experiences of diverse students and promotes more thought to strategies that acknowledge those experiences.

Bensimon (2007) suggests that practitioners do not see themselves as agents of student success for marginalized groups because they lack the funds of knowledge and expertise to recognize the racialized nature of students' experiences and adjust their practices accordingly. We recommend the use of Bensimon's practitioner-researcher model to address this knowledge gap and to raise awareness of achievement inequalities. Over time, practitioner and researchers become more knowledgeable by examining the evidence in context (classrooms, learning centers, program initiatives, informal interactions) and become more equity-minded by discussing performance data disaggregated by race and ethnicity. Expert assistance may be required to uncover biases and attitudes resistant to change and to bring practitioners to the point at which they raise the kinds of questions that assist them in reaching their students, such as, "What are we doing that is working or not working with minority students? How can we be more successful?"

Faculty and Staff-Student Interaction. Research from the Community College Survey of Student Engagement tells us that student engagement is about relationship and that interactions are most likely when faculty and students are in the same place, the classroom. To promote large-scale utilization of promising relational practices, we suggest faculty and staff institute learning communities, career mentoring, collaborative research projects, and authentic problem-based learning activities. Validating students by inviting them into collegiate relationships affirms that they belong, encourages confidence, and builds social and cultural capital.

Professional Development for Senior Administrators. Opportunities for senior administrators to enhance their ability to manage the cultural dimensions of their institutions emanate from a qualitative research perspective. Activities help participants audit the alignment of the core mission and values with the organization's structure, policies, practices, and budget. They focus on the various student populations served by the institution and on the possibilities for increasing student success. Two strategies that we would like to highlight are the equity scorecard and appreciative inquiry.

Equity Scorecard. Bensimon (2005) recommends that the academic leadership use an equity scorecard as a vehicle for the institution to assess itself by examining, and more importantly, understanding the performance data of its various student subpopulations and identifying indicators or benchmarks to measure the impact of its interventions. The equity measures become a major way the institution holds individuals and the collective body accountable.

Bensimon suggests that administrators, faculty, and support staff form evidence-based communities to discuss any inequities uncovered by the data. This creates the opportunity to uncover, challenge, and change attitudes, beliefs, assumptions, and practices and move from deficit (blaming the student) and diversity (promoting cross-racial understanding) frameworks to an equity framework (examining unequal results). In the equity framework, the focus is on how the institution and particularly individuals create a culture in the classrooms and other units of the institution. This culture would respond to the needs of all students and especially their values and would seriously react to underserved students to whom we have the responsibility to see that they succeed—at a minimum to a percentage that is proportional to their representation in the institution.

Appreciative Inquiry. An approach that has become a popular change method is appreciative inquiry (AI). In this approach developed by Cooperrider and Srivasta (1987), the assumption is that every organization is doing something right when it is working at its best. It addresses such questions as, "What is the institution like when it is most successful?" Moreover, "How do we sustain successful practices?" AI is possibility focused rather than problem focused, so it inspires creative and positive energy among constituents. Based in the theory of social constructionism, the AI model includes the four phases of discovery, dream, design, and delivery. Watkins and Mohr (2001) describe five generic processes of AI and link them with the four phases originally proposed by Cooperider and Srivasta: (1) choosing the positive as the focus of inquiry (definition), (2) inquiring into stories of life-giving forces (discovery), (3) locating themes that appear in the stories and selecting topics for further inquiry (discovery), (4) creating shared images for a preferred future (dream), and (5) finding innovative ways to create that future (design and delivery).

A useful resource for senior leaders is Stetson and Miller's (2004) summary of ten case studies of community colleges that have effectively used AI to effect institutional change. One of those colleges, Harrisburg Area Community College, adopted AI to create student-focused learning partnerships across one of its campuses and to strengthen cooperative partnerships college-wide starting with its twelve top administrators. The experience moved the cabinet members away from a competitive culture to an appreciation of one another's contributions to a cooperative and student-focused organization. Organizational priorities and practices were brought in line with this new vision.

The underlying orientation for all of these recommendations could be categorized as a kind of *minding the mind-set*. We must understand who we are as an institution inclusive of all its members, align this understanding with our practices, and continually reflect on the interplay between the two as we make decisions about policies, resources, and interventions in response to our evolving cultural awareness, the equity effects of our actions, and our students' experience of our efforts. As institutional leaders, faculty, and staff, we must guard against the rationale that lack of student preparation, lack of motivation, and neighborhood environments are formidable barriers beyond our control. Certainly they have an impact, as do all of the experiences students bring to a situation, but we can decide to respond by looking within our institutions as enablers of student success and creating safe environments for students to reconcile familiar and new contexts as they make the transition to the academic culture.

References

Arbona, C., and Nora, A. "The Influence of Academic and Environmental Factors on Hispanic College Degree Attainment." *Review of Higher Education,* 2007, *30*(3), 247–269.

Bensimon, E. M. *Equality as a Fact, Equality as a Result: A Matter of Institutional Accountability.* Washington, D.C.: American Council on Education, 2005.

Bensimon, E. M. "The Underestimated Significance of Practitioner Knowledge in the Scholarship on Student Success." *Review of Higher Education,* 2007, *30*(4), 441–469.

Berger, P., and Luckman, T. *The Social Construction of Reality.* New York: Anchor, 1967.

Chickering, A. W., and Gamson, C. F. "Seven Principles for Good Practice in Undergraduate Education." *AAHE Bulletin,* 1987, *39*(7), 3–7.

NEW DIRECTIONS FOR COMMUNITY COLLEGES • DOI: 10.1002/cc

Collins, J. *Good to Great.* New York: HarperCollins, 2001.

Cooperrider, D., and Srivasta, S. "Appreciative Inquiry in Organizational Life." In W. Pasmore and R. Woodman (eds.), *Research in Organizational Change and Development.* Greenwich, Conn.: JAI Press, 1987.

Eckel, P. D., and Kezar, A. *Taking the Reins: Institutional Transformation in Higher Education.* Westport, Conn.: Praeger, 2003.

Education Commission of the States. *Making Quality Count in Undergraduate Education.* Denver, Colo.: Education Commission of the States, 1995.

Hurtado, S., and Carter, D. F. "Effects of College Transition and Perceptions of the Campus Racial Climate on Latino College Students' Sense of Belonging." *Sociology of Education,* 1997, 70(4), 324–345.

Kuh, G., Kinzie, J., Schuh, J., and Whitt, E. *Student Success in College: Creating Conditions That Matter.* San Francisco: Jossey-Bass, 2005.

Kuh, G., and Whitt, E. *The Invisible Tapestry: Culture in American Colleges and Universities.* ASHE-ERIC Higher Education Report, No. 1. Washington, D.C.: Association for the Study of Higher Education, 1988.

Lazarus, R. *Emotion and Adaptation.* New York: Oxford University Press, 1991.

McGrath, D., and Van Buskirk, W. *Crafting a Culture of Success for Women Engineers.* Philadelphia: LaSalle University, Nonprofit Management Development Center, 1993.

McGrath, D., and Van Buskirk, W. *Si Se Puede: The Summer Scholars Transfer Institute: Collaborating to Promote Access and Achievement.* Philadelphia: LaSalle University, Nonprofit Development Center, 1998.

McGrath, D., and Van Buskirk, W. *The ACE Advantage: Charting the Pathway from High School to College.* Philadelphia: LaSalle University, Nonprofit Management Development Center, 1999.

McLeod, W. B., and Young, J. M. "A Chancellor's Vision: Establishing an Institutional Culture of Student Success." In G. H Gaither (ed.), *Minority Retention: What Works?* New Directions for Institutional Research, no. 125. San Francisco: Jossey-Bass, 2005.

McPhail, C. J., and Costner, K. L. "Seven Principles for Training a Culturally Responsive Faculty." *Learning Abstracts,* 2004, 7(12), 1–6.

Morgan, P., Frost, P. J., and Pondy, L. R. "Organizational Symbolism." In L. R. Pondy, P. J. Frost, G. Morgan, and T. C. Dandridge (eds.), *Organizational Symbolism.* Greenwich, Conn.: JAI, 1983.

Nieto, S. "Lessons from Students on Creating a Chance to Dream." *Harvard Educational Review,* 1994, 64(4), 25–59.

Nora, A. "Determinants of Retention Among Chicano College Students: A Structural Model." *Research in Higher Education,* 1987, 26(1), 31–59.

Nora, A. "Access to Higher Education for Hispanic Students: Real or Illusory?" In J. Castellanos and L. Jones (eds.), *The Majority in the Minority: Expanding Representation of Latino/a Faculty, Administration and Students in Higher Education.* Sterling, Va.: Stylus Publishing, 2003.

Nora, A., and Cabrera, A. F. "The Role of Perceptions of Prejudice and Discrimination on the Adjustment of Minority Students to College." *Journal of Higher Education,* 1996, 67(2), 119–148.

Rendón, L. I. "Transforming the First-Year Experience for Students of Color: Where Do We Begin?" In L. I. Rendón, M. García, and D. Person (eds.), *Transforming the First Year of College for Students of Color.* Columbia, S.C.: University of South Carolina, National Resource Center for the First-Year Experience and Students in Transition, 2004.

Rendón, L. I., García, M., and Person, D. (eds.). *Transforming the First Year of College for Students of Color.* Columbia, S.C.: University of South Carolina, National Resource Center for the First-Year Experience and Students in Transition, 2004.

Rendón, L. I., and Hope, R. O. (eds.). *Educating a New Majority: Transforming America's Educational System for Diversity.* San Francisco: Jossey-Bass, 1996.

Schein, E. H. *Organizational Culture and Leadership.* San Francisco: Jossey-Bass, 1985.

Schein, E. H. *Organizational Culture and Leadership.* (2nd ed.) San Francisco: Jossey-Bass, 1992.

Shaw, K., and London, H. "Culture and Ideology in Keeping Transfer Commitment: Three Community Colleges." *Review of Higher Education,* 2001, 25(1), 91–114.

Stetson, N. E., and Miller, C. R. *Appreciative Inquiry in the Community College: Early Stories of Success.* Phoenix, Ariz.: League for Innovation in the Community College, 2004.

Study Group on the Conditions of Excellence in American Higher Education. *Involvement in Learning.* Washington, D.C.: U.S. Department of Education, 1984.

Swidler, A. "Culture in Action: Symbols and Strategies." *American Sociological Review,* 1986, 51(2), 273–286.

Tinto, V., Goodsell, A., and Russo, P. *Building Learning Communities for New College Students.* Philadelphia: Pennsylvania State University, National Center on Postsecondary Teaching, Learning, and Assessment, 1994.

Watkins, J. M., and Mohr, B. J. *Appreciative Inquiry.* San Francisco: Jossey-Bass, 2001.

Weick, K. E. *Sensemaking in Organizations.* Thousand Oaks, Calif.: Sage, 1995.

DENNIS MCGRATH *is professor of sociology at the Community College of Philadelphia.*

SUSAN TOBIA *is executive assistant to the vice president for academic affairs at the Community College of Philadelphia.*

This chapter presents an overview of a new tiered mentoring program operating at Bellevue Community College in Washington. The program links students with peers, faculty, staff, and administrators via a tiered structure whereby first-year students are mentored by upper-level students, who in turn are mentored by professionals in the students' field of study.

Tiered Mentoring to Leverage Student Body Expertise

Faisal Jaswal, Teresa McClane Jaswal

It is fair to say that community colleges have a unique challenge in reaching students in a deep, meaningful way from the first day that they set foot on campuses until the day that they graduate. Although most community colleges have variations of a new student orientation, freshman experience, or other types of welcoming and integrating programs, the fact remains that many new students do not make a connection from the start of their college experience. In addition, most colleges have variations of student retention programs and mentoring components; nevertheless, many students are left untouched by these programs.

Retention research shows that the earlier a student is connected to the social and academic systems of the college the greater their academic achievement and thus their commitment to graduating (Astin, 1993; Milem and Berger, 1997; Pascarella, Smart, and Ethington, 1986). Significant money and staffing are needed to operate such programs, but colleges are faced with reduced governmental resources, budget cuts, and unmet staffing needs. One solution is to establish a tiered mentoring program (TMP), which includes a peer-mentoring component. One of the earliest peer-mentoring programs was established at James Cook University (Queensland, Australia) in 1991. Treston (1999) reports supporting new students in a context of shrinking government resources and increased workloads for staff as a primary motivation for its introduction (Freeman and Kelton, 2004). The tiered peer-mentoring program (TMP) at Bellevue Community

NEW DIRECTIONS FOR COMMUNITY COLLEGES, no. 144, Winter 2008 © 2008 Wiley Periodicals, Inc.
Published online in Wiley InterScience (www.interscience.wiley.com) • DOI: 10.1002/cc.345

College in Washington is outlined within this chapter. The TMP is designed to be sustainable and scalable to eventually reach all students at the college.

Background

Bellevue Community College (BCC) sits on the edge of Lake Washington, approximately twenty miles to the east of Seattle and near Microsoft's corporate headquarters. BCC is a single campus and serves thirty-five thousand students each year. The student population has diverse and varying needs. Many students work as well as attend school, and the challenge has been to retain students by making interactions meaningful and personalized.

First Days of a Term

Envision the first three days of a BCC quarter. New and continuing students fill every square foot of the grounds, corridors, and, in particular, the student services building. The building is a collision of registration, financial aid, cashiering, the bookstore, advising, counseling, career services, multicultural services, evaluation, high school programs, and international student programs.

To watch the first three days of a BCC quarter from the second floor of the student services building is something reminiscent of the New York Stock Exchange. It proves the point that there must be relevancy to the organizational chaos theory. People are moving through the narrow passages between the lines of people waiting to get into the bookstore or to be served at the student services counter. The din fills the air and wafts upward until the walls reverberate. Students may wait in one of these many lines to find out that the book that they need has not arrived or that they did not reach the student services counter in time to register for the class that they were next on the waitlist for. They may find they cannot register for their class because there is a block on their registration. Other students may not be able to find their classroom or the instructor who is supposed to be teaching the class. The situational list is never-ending and unpredictable. At BCC, it takes kind and helpful souls numerous hours to try to answer every question, help every lost student, process every class change and bookstore need, complete every monetary transaction, and solve every crisis. Are the first days of your quarter or semester similar?

Recognizing the challenges associated with the first week of class, BCC's student programs office and a group of dedicated, seasoned students created the TMP. As a result, TMP student mentors decreased the amount of time students were standing in line, provided answers to many of the students' questions, helped lost students find their classrooms and instructors, lent an empathetic ear to hear their frustrations, and shared these concerns with BCC leaders. They offered a friendly face to help make the first few days of school less alienating and overwhelming. Consequently, BCC has

New Directions for Community Colleges • DOI: 10.1002/cc

been moving away from new student orientations as the sole forum for distributing information and moving towards more interactive social exchanges such as the TMP, where new students can begin to make connections to the college (Bennett and Jaswal, 2007a).

Tiered Mentoring Program

In the past, BCC has piloted new student mentoring programs and industry mentoring programs for smaller groups of students. These programs have been successful for the small percentages of the student population that they serve, but are difficult to sustain or expand without appropriate funding and dedicated staffing. The TMP strives to transition all new students during their first quarter at BCC by connecting them with academic and support services, while establishing a social connection with seasoned students. New students are provided with a campus tour and introduced to student programs; the library; the tutoring center; writing, reading, and math labs; educational planning; financial aid; the Center for Career Connections; the Women's Center; and multicultural services. Likewise, TMP student mentors are connected with staff and faculty and increasingly are connected with industry professionals in their fields of study. The TMP goal is to serve every new student for fall, winter, and spring quarters.

By serving new students and modeling the behavior it takes to be an academically successful student, the TMP student mentors develop leadership skills. TMP student mentors provide guidance, support, friendship, and connection to the college that otherwise would be nonexistent to the majority of the new student population. This program is unique in that it is provided to every new student and encourages students to help other students, thus promoting a new campus culture that fosters collegiality and collaboration (Bennett and Jaswal, 2007a).

Training. Before they work with new students, TMP student mentors are provided with comprehensive training to gain the knowledge, skills, and abilities to become effective mentors. During their training, TMP student mentors develop leadership skills and competencies, learn about their role in the college community and in the matriculation and retention process, learn about the role of the mentee, and establish mentoring relationships with campus or community members. Within the training, specific learning objectives have been developed. Mentors are expected to explain the role of TMP student mentors, list several helping positions on the college campus that are staffed by TMP student mentors, understand and employ an active process model of learning, explain the importance of role modeling within the helping role, define the role of a mentor and a mentee, and assess their ability to serve in both the mentoring and mentee relationship. This training focuses on issues that are relevant to an understanding of the transitional needs of students entering or returning to the college setting. Key topics covered are BCC's mission, vision, and values; servant leadership;

cross-cultural competency; effective communication; team building; strategies for academic success; and BCC's campus resources (Bennett and Jaswal, 2007b).

Expectations. Attendance, participation, and preparedness are essential to the success of the program. TMP student mentors are expected to attend trainings, keep scheduled mentoring hours, be prepared for meetings with mentees, and be available to participate in planned mentor program activities and recruitment initiatives. They assist with quarterly new student orientations, help new students during the first three days of school, complete quarterly phone calls to new students, and promote other program recruitment and outreach activities. In addition, TMP student mentors are required to be available, accountable, and authentic in each of their interactions, ensuring that new students have a positive experience (Bennett and Jaswal, 2007b).

The TMP is designed to work collaboratively with other student support services on-campus. The TMP student mentors act as a conduit, referring students to academic, financial, and social resources on campus. In addition, the TMP can support other departments by providing student mentors when their programming requires. For example, TMP student mentors assist educational planning advisors as part of their advising model. By working collaboratively with other departments, the TMP enables other departments to enhance their current programming without duplicity.

Budget. The TMP was piloted with funding from both the leadership institute and new student orientation budgets under the services and activities fees. All the aforementioned programs are located in and operated by the student programs office. Initially, TMP student mentors volunteered their time because they believed it was important to connect to new students and wished that they had received the same benefit when they were new students. However, BCC felt it important that the TMP student mentors be compensated and were able to secure a small amount of funding to cover the expense. Compensation is critical to the continued ability to recruit and retrain motivated, qualified TMP student mentors (Bennett and Jaswal, 2007a).

Coordination. The TMP requires two dedicated student coordinators who work a combined twenty-six hours per week and one permanent staff member who contributes a quarter of his or her time to provide oversight and training. There are over one-hundred fifty student mentors registered in the program. The TMP is self-perpetuating; students who were initially helped as new students often feel motivated and empowered to do the same. For example, two current TMP student mentors were contacted as new students during the first quarter phone calls. The two students were so grateful that someone had reached out to them that they wanted to be part of the program and help others. In addition, TMP student mentors are recruited through our Honor Society chapter, student government, other student organizations, and clubs. Diversity in student mentors and student leadership is extremely important to reflect the diversity of BCC's student population; the TMP student mentors and student program's staff especially reach out to diverse students to ask them to serve. These student leaders provide a steady pool of strong role models for newer students. Quarterly training and orientation of TMP student mentors, evaluation, and data collection are integral components of the TMP. TMP student mentor and new student concerns and issues are recorded and follow-up is conducted.

Results. From summer quarter 2006 through winter quarter 2007, TMP student mentors volunteered over one thousand hours and assisted 12,670 students. During winter quarter 2007, seventeen TMP student mentors called over five hundred new students to welcome them, assist with questions, discuss online orientation, or schedule time to meet for a personal orientation and a campus tour (Bennett and Jaswal, 2007a). During fall quarter 2007 and winter quarter 2008, three groups of new students who enrolled in ten or more credits each quarter were compared: students who enrolled without advising and contact by TMP student mentors were retained at 69.6 percent, students who enrolled with advising, but without contact by TMP student mentors were retained at 72.6 percent; and students who enrolled with advising and with phone contact by TMP student mentors were retained at 81.4 percent. Although this initial data collection did not control for student background or other institutional factors, further data collection is being conducted to gather more conclusive results.

Next Steps. Electronic channels are increasingly the medium of choice for students to communicate and interact with the TMP student mentors and vice versa. In the near future, BCC will implement electronic social networking channels to better serve the millennial student population and nontraditional student populations who need the flexibility provided by online tools.

Networking. One of the final tiers of the TMP, which is to connect TMP student mentors to industry professionals in their fields of study, has been initiated. A collaborative pilot between the BCC student program's office, the center for career connections, and the women's center, will be conducted fall quarter 2008 with ten of the TMP student mentors. Industry mentors will be identified, trained, and matched to each of the ten TMP student mentors. It is anticipated that each mentor and mentee will meet in-person two to three times during the course of three months. Materials and resources will be used from BCC's experiential learning class (EXPRL 230), including job shadowing and professional networking activities with brief manual and podcasts developed for both mentors and mentees to establish guidelines and help facilitate the process and interactions. In addition, e-portfolios and cocurricular transcripts will be created for TMP student mentors.

Lastly, the center for Career Connections and the Women's Center plans to create and initiate an online mentoring system available to all students to virtually connect with industry professionals in their fields of interest. Industry professionals will be contacted and asked to volunteer their time to mentor students through BCC's online career management system, CONNECT! Students will be able to self-select mentors and contact them via e-mail a controlled number of times. To date, there has been tremendous interest expressed by industry professionals at organizations such as Boeing, Microsoft, and the Bellevue Rotary.

Conclusion

There have been many lessons learned from initiating the tiered mentoring program at Bellevue College. First, TMP appears to foster success of new students, in itself a worthy accomplishment. In addition, because many new students confide concerns or issues to TMP student mentors that they might not feel comfortable sharing with faculty or staff, TMP offers a new and powerful perspective on students' early campus experiences. In fact, TMP student mentors have become the eyes and ears of the campus, helping to highlight obstacles facing new students that might otherwise go unnoticed.

Furthermore, the TMP is a remarkably flexible structure that can be adapted to serve students with various levels of funding. For example, at BCC, it was important to start small and grow the program each year. Similarly, other colleges may find that starting with one tier or one portion of a tier can help make initiating a TMP seem less daunting and more feasible. New tiers or components can be added as the program grows and using technology tools can help reach larger numbers of students.

Funding may not be initially provided to the program, so beginning with TMP student mentor volunteers may be necessary until a small amount of funding can be secured. It is important to stay positive and be creative when exploring funding options. Funding could potentially come from services and activities fees, from benefiting departments each contributing a small portion of funding to the TMP, from the campus' foundation, or from other sources. Most important, TMP student mentors are well intentioned, but they still have to factor in an amount of time that they can serve while balancing school and work demands. It is recommended that faculty or staff overseeing the student mentors provide guidance to help student mentors avoid overextension.

In conclusion, initiating and sustaining a TMP does take effort, but the benefits of creating more opportunities for students to succeed far outweighs the additional work. At BCC, the power of mentoring relationships has been glimpsed and experienced. By initiating the TMP, the college is working toward a more connected, vibrant campus. As more tiers of the TMP are added, a cultural shift is anticipated not only on the campus, but also in the greater community. By helping students connect with students, students connect with staff and faculty, and students connect with industry professionals, people are empowered and better able to succeed. A stronger community is created. From a philosophical point of view, that is really the beauty of the community college system: community.

References

Astin, A. W. *What Matters in College? Four Critical Years Revisited.* San Francisco: Jossey-Bass, 1993.

Bennett, G., and Jaswal, F. *Peer-to-Peer Mentoring Program Goals and Objectives.* Bellevue, Wash.: Bellevue Community College, 2007a.

Bennett, G., and Jaswal, F. *Peer-to-Peer Mentor Program Training.* Bellevue, Wash.: Bellevue Community College, 2007b.

Freeman, M., and Kelton, J. "Peer Mentoring Programs: Enhancing the Learning Experience in Economics and Business." *Synergy,* 2004, *20,* 29–31. Accessed Aug. 19, 2008, at http://www.itl.usyd.edu.au/synergy/synergy20.pdf.

Milem, J. F., and Berger, J. B. "A Modified Model of College Student Persistence: Exploring the Relationship Between Astin's Theory of Involvement and Tinto's Theory of Student Departure." *Journal of College Student Development,* 1997, *38*(4), 387–399.

Pascarella, E. T., Smart, J. C., and Ethington, C. A. "Long-Term Persistence of Two-Year College Students." *Research in Higher Education,* 1986, *24*(1), 47–71.

Treston, H. "Shifting Paradigms in Mentoring Programmes in Higher Education." Paper presented at the Second Regional Conference on Tutoring and Mentoring, Perth, Australia, Oct. 1999. Accessed Aug. 19, 2008, at http://about.murdoch.edu.au/star/conference_proceedings/proceedings.html.

FAISAL JASWAL is assistant dean of student programs at Bellevue Community College in Bellevue, Washington.

TERESA MCCLANE JASWAL is assistant director of the Center for Career Connections and the Women's Center at Bellevue Community College in Bellevue, Washington.

This chapter explores institutional attributes that matter for two-year college students and how they vary by different subpopulations of students, with an eye toward understanding what institutional attributes better support the success of underprepared students.

Do Institutional Attributes Predict Individuals' Degree Success at Two-Year Colleges?

Lisbeth J. Goble, James E. Rosenbaum, Jennifer L. Stephan

Although American society has made great gains in the numbers and proportion of high school students attending community college over the last several decades, actual completion rates have remained low (Hoachlander, Sikora, and Horn, 2003). Most research on students' college success has centered on the influence of individual attributes such as socioeconomic status, race, and prior achievement (Alexander and Eckland, 1975; Hearn, 1988; Pascarella and Terenzini, 2005; Sewell and Shah, 1967). However, the idea that certain institutional attributes can have a systemic influence on student success at two-year colleges is emerging in recent studies (Rosenbaum, Deil-Amen, and Person, 2006).

Titus (2004) and Bailey and others (2005) are two of the few studies that examine whether institutional attributes contribute to student success after controlling for individual attributes, although only the latter focuses on two-year colleges. The current study builds upon prior work by including an institutional measure proposed by accountability advocates, but empirically overlooked in models of individual degree completion: institutional graduation rate. We find a positive association between individual completion and institutional graduation rate for the entire sample, but variation across subgroups of students. We also find significant associations between individual completion and college size, the proportion of part-time faculty, and the proportion of minority students.

NEW DIRECTIONS FOR COMMUNITY COLLEGES, no. 144, Winter 2008 © 2008 Wiley Periodicals, Inc.
Published online in Wiley InterScience (www.interscience.wiley.com) • DOI: 10.1002/cc.346

Institutional graduation rate is defined by the U.S. Department of Education as the percentage of full-time, first-time students in an entering cohort who complete their degrees within 150 percent of the expected time (three years for associate degrees). As public policy's focus in higher education has shifted from blaming students to holding institutions accountable for student outcomes, at least thirty-six states have implemented policies tying college resources to institutional graduation rates (Dougherty and Hong, 2006). However, there has been no systematic assessment of the usefulness of institutions' aggregate graduation rates as predictors of community college student outcomes across different groups of students.

Given the diversity of community college students, it is likely that certain college attributes will matter for degree completion for some subgroups of students, but not for others. For instance, it is possible that the proportion of full-time faculty only influence students who go to see faculty after class hours, and that small schools mostly benefit students who need closer attention. Even among full-time and first-time college students, the average graduation rate for a particular institution may not predict an *individual* student's degree completion, especially for students at different levels of achievement.

To illustrate, consider that a college with a 50 percent graduation rate and a bimodal distribution may have a 75 percent graduation rate for high-achieving students and a 25 percent graduation rate for low-achieving students, with only a few students represented by the calculated institutional graduation rate of 50 percent. Furthermore, institutional graduation rate calculations neglect a large population of community college students, such as those who enroll part time or those who take long interruptions before reenrolling. In sum, it appears that we know very little about what institutional attributes matter to which groups of students. This information seems necessary before using institutional attributes to assess institutional accountability.

This chapter examines which institutional factors predict individual community college student success, whether this accountability indicator is a useful addition, and whether the indicator varies across students with different levels of academic preparation. In particular, this chapter addresses the following questions:

1. Which institutional attributes are associated with students' degree completion at two-year colleges?
2. Does college graduation rate have a significant impact in predicting degree completion beyond what one could predict from just knowing those institutional attributes?
3. Does college graduation rate remain a predictor of individual degree completion after controlling for students' individual attributes?
4. Do institutional attributes, including graduation rate, provide useful information for students at all levels of achievement or only for certain subgroups?

Given that focusing on a single outcome indicator could create unintended consequences (for example, excluding at-risk students who may hurt the college's graduation rates), research needs to show that the graduation rate provides useful information beyond other institutional attributes that students can already use. It also needs to show whether graduation rates are influential net of individual attributes, and whether it is so for different subgroups of students. To date, research has largely neglected these issues, which are the focus of this chapter.

Sample and Methods

This study uses the National Education Longitudinal Study Restricted Use File (NELS: 88–00) to examine the predictors of college degree completion. The baseline NELS sample was drawn from the universe of students enrolled in the eighth grade during the 1988–1989 school year. Follow-ups were conducted in 1990, 1992, 1994, and 2000. The sample was refreshed in tenth and twelfth grades to be representative of those grades at that time. Using the *f4f2pnwt* sample weights provided in the NELS data set, this analysis is representative of U.S. students who were in the twelfth grade in 1992.

The analytical sample is limited to students who intend to earn associate's degrees or higher and first enroll in a degree-granting two-year college. Furthermore, we include only those students who enroll in college immediately after high school and report being enrolled full-time for the duration of their college career, and we allow them up to eight years to complete a degree (associate's or higher). Consequently, these analyses present a best-case scenario for degree completion by focusing on the students to whom the institutional graduation rate most closely applies and allowing them eight years for degree completion. The current analysis used list-wise deletion of cases resulting in a sample size of 1,067 students.

To account for institutional attributes, the NELS data were merged with data from the Integrated Postsecondary Education Data System (IPEDS). One shortcoming of prior studies of institutional effects is that they rely on student-reported measures of their institutions' characteristics. The IPEDS data provide a direct measure of specific institutional attributes. IPEDS data are collected annually and contain information on enrollment, completion, staffing, and finance for all providers of postsecondary education in the United States. Individual-level data from NELS were merged with institutional-level IPEDS data from 1992–1993 unless otherwise noted.

One benefit to using the NELS data over other data with college-going samples such as the Beginning Post-Secondary Study is the availability of twelfth-grade achievement scores for over three-quarters of the sample. For those missing twelfth-grade test scores, tenth-grade scores were used, and if both were missing, eighth-grade scores were used (twelfth-grade test scores are highly correlated with eighth- and tenth-grade scores, $r = .85$ and $r = .91$, respectively). This resulted in nearly 98 percent of the sample having test score data and reduced the overall bias of the sample from list-wise deletion. To examine completion rates associated with levels of academic preparation, the analytical sample was split into thirds based on the composite math and reading score.

Dependent Variable. The dependent variable is completion of any degree, associate's or higher, within eight years of finishing high school.

Independent Variables. Independent variables fall into two broad categories, individual and institutional characteristics. These were selected according to which prominent models of postsecondary persistence are identified as important to student success and also with an eye toward some of the central concerns in today's college choice discussions (Bean 1982; Braxton, Hirschy, and McClendon, 2004; Pascarella and Terenzini, 2005; Tinto, 1993). Individual-level variables include demographic characteristics such as gender, race or ethnicity, and family socioeconomic status, as well as high school achievement and urbanicity of their high school (urban, suburban, or rural).

Besides an institution's graduation rate, we use institutional variables from three broad categories studied in prior research (Bailey and others, 2005): compositional, institutional, and organizational. Compositional variables reflect the student-body composition and include total fall undergraduate enrollment, percentage of fall undergraduates enrolled part time, and the percentage of students who are members of a racial or ethnic minority group. Institutional variables include dummy variables for private (versus public) status and urbanicity of the college. Organizational variables reflect these two-year colleges' policies and practices and include the percentage of faculty who are part-time employees, whether the college provides dormitories, whether it requires an admissions test, and a composite spending ratio composed of spending on academic, administrative, instructional, and student services (Pascarella and Terenzini, 2005).

For both methodological and theoretical reasons, institutional characteristics are measured only for the first institution where the student enrolled. Almost 50 percent of students in the sample change colleges at least once during the course of their postsecondary careers. Some go on to complete higher degrees, but some are still working on their first degree when they switch institutions. Rather than excluding these students from our analyses, we chose to examine the effects of their initial college experiences on their chances of completing the degree. Following other theorists (Bean, 1982; Tinto, 1993), we contend that the first year influences the trajectory of students' later college careers, depending on the formative experiences and social integration provided. Moreover, policymakers largely focus on the question of improving the initial choices of high school seniors; there is no discussion about policies to improve the college choices of students changing colleges.

Descriptive statistics for the analytical sample are available from the authors upon request. Dividing students into three equal categories based on high school academic achievement, this chapter examines the determinants of individual degree completion in community colleges for each third as well as for the total. As one would expect, students with higher levels of high school achievement complete degrees at higher rates (62 percent for high achievers, 49 percent for middle achievers, 37 percent for low achievers, and 45 percent for the complete sample). However, although students in these three groups attend community colleges with similar average graduation rates (23 to 25 percent), the institutional graduation rate varies considerably within each group (with standard deviations ranging from 12 to 15).

Using binary logistic regression, model one in this analysis examines how much variation in individual degree completion can be explained by available institutional attributes. Then model two examines whether students would get any additional useful information by considering graduation rate beyond the indicators already available. Finally, model three examines whether institutional or graduation rate indicators enhance prediction over and above students' own attributes. The analysis is repeated for subgroups of high, middle, and low-achieving students to see if the process works differently for different kinds of students. We adjust for sampling design with Stata 9.0 SE (StataCorp, 2005) survey and subpopulation commands.

Results

First, we present the results for the full sample of two-year college students, and we then look at the three achievement subgroups to see what variation, if any, exists for the high, middle, and low-achieving students in our sample. Table 6.1 summarizes the significant findings for each analytical group. The full results are available from the authors.

Complete Sample. In our analysis of all students who start at two-year colleges, we find that students with higher high school achievement have higher odds of completing an associate's degree or higher. We also find that there is, in fact, a positive and significant impact of the institution's graduation rate on students' odds of degree completion. All else being equal, attending a college with a one point higher graduation rate increases the odds of individual completion by a little more than three percentage points. This finding supports accountability advocates' calls for improving institutional graduation rates. As we will see, however, this finding does not apply to most students.

In addition to graduation rate, we find other institutional impacts on individual degree completion. A larger proportion of minority students enrolled in the college has a negative influence on a student's chances of graduating. The college's use of an admission test also has a negative impact on student's odds of degree completion, although the significance of this goes away once individual attributes are accounted for in the models. We suggest possible interpretations below, but overall find only a few institutional attributes significant for the complete sample of students.

Table 6.1. Summary of Logistic Regression of Individual College Degree Completion on Individual and Institutional Characteristics by Achievement Subgroups *(direction of effect in parentheses)*

	Complete Sample	High Achievers	Middle Achievers	Low Achievers
Graduation Rate	Yes	No	Yes	No
Other Institutional Attributes	Percent Minority Student (–) School Size: 1,000–2,500 (+) Admissions Test Required (–)	Percent Part-time Faculty (–) School Size: 2,500–5,000 (+) 10k–15k (+)	Suburban (+) School Size: Less than 1,000 (+)	Percent Minority Students (–)
Individual Attributes	High School Achievement (+) American Indian/ Alaska Native (+)	—	Female (+)	High School Achievement (+) Asian-Pacific Islander (+) American Indian/ Alaska Native (+)

High Achievers. For the high achievers, the institutional graduation rate no longer has an impact on student degree completion. Instead, we find a few institutional variables that were not significant for all students now reaching significance for high-achieving students. Most notably, students who attend schools with higher proportions of part-time faculty have significantly reduced odds of completing their degree.

In addition, we find that school size matters. Students who attend mid-sized schools (2,500–5,000 and 10,000–15,000 student enrollments) have significantly higher rates of degree completion than those in schools with over 15,000 students. Interestingly, for these students, we do not find any impact of individual attributes on degree completion.

Middle Achievers. When examining our middle achievers, we find diverging patterns from both the complete sample and high achievers. In these models, we find several institutional variables that are important in predicting degree completion. Middle-achieving students in suburban colleges do significantly better than those attending urban schools. Although high-achieving students do better in midsized colleges, mid-achieving students do better in small (and sometimes midsized) schools compared to those in large colleges. We find a slightly negative, but significant, impact of spending on students. This is a crude measure, perhaps reflecting school spending on remediation services, but further exploration into this finding is needed.

We also find that the middle achievers seem to be driving much of the impact of graduation rates seen in the complete sample. Of the three subgroups, this is the only one where institutional graduation rate has a statistically significant association with individuals' outcomes, perhaps suggesting that graduation rate is important to consider for these individuals but not others.

Low Achievers. For the lowest third of students, the percentage of minority students enrolled at the school negatively influences individual degree completion. This is the only institutional variable that is significant in the full model and is driving the finding for the complete sample. Beyond this, these models find no influences of institutional indicators. Of the three subgroups, this is the only one where we see impacts of several individual attributes, including Asian and Native American ethnicity and prior achievement. Although it is not surprising that students with relatively higher prior achievement do better, it is surprising that this only occurs for the lowest group of students. There is considerable variation in achievement within all three groups, but this variation affects degree completion only in the lowest group.

Discussion

These analyses provide considerable support to the hypothesis that institutional attributes matter in student outcomes. However, we also find that institutional graduation rate does not hold up very well when examined empirically in the context of community colleges. Contrary to those who advocate for the use of institutional graduation rates as a predictor of success, we find that this indicator has no association with chances of completing a degree for students from the top or bottom thirds of achievement. Thus, it is unlikely that this indicator identifies institutional impact on individual students or that this criterion would offer much predictive power over outcomes beyond information contained in other institutional variables.

What about influences of other institutional indicators such as school size and proportion of full-time faculty? Everyone knows that the same factor can have different impacts on different kinds of individuals. We speculated above that full-time faculty may only matter to students who go to see faculty after class hours, and small schools may mostly benefit students needing closer attention. Interestingly, in these analyses we find that small colleges only benefit midachieving students, and midsized colleges only benefit the top-achieving students. Although both groups do worse at the largest colleges, college size has no impact on the lowest-achieving students. Even if small and middle-sized colleges have greater capacity for assisting students, this smaller size may assist middle- and high-achieving students, but it is not sufficient to affect the outcomes of low-achieving students.

We also find that a higher proportion of part-time faculty has a negative impact, but only for the high-achieving group. Although we can speculate that part-time faculty do not harm other groups because such students do not seek their help, the mechanism requires further study. However, these results clearly indicate such relationships deserve to be investigated and point to new directions for further research to examine how institutional attributes might have these effects. Practically, they suggest the possibility that though community colleges have been pushed to reduce full-time faculty to cut costs, these reductions may be hurting student outcomes, particularly for higher achieving students. Detailed institutional studies are needed to examine why these factors have an impact, what other institutional factors might be important, and why some factors have different impacts for different kinds of students.

The most puzzling finding from this study is the much lower individual degree completion in colleges with high proportions of minorities. Are these colleges deprived of key resources, poorly administered, or politically neglected? Or are they located in neighborhoods with high poverty rates, which have negative impacts such as anxieties arising from deprivation and crime (Wilson, 1996)? We cannot answer these questions; nevertheless, the results show that this is only a problem for low-achieving students.

Limitations

These findings were based on data for students with degree plans of an associate's degree or higher who first enroll in a degree-granting, two-year college immediately after high school. Therefore, findings may not generalize to students who are older, attending less than full-time, or are undecided about their educational objectives. These students are likely to take much longer and to have lower degree completion rates (Bozick and Deluca, 2005; Hearn, 1992).

Furthermore, although it is impressive to have institutional information from IPEDS, these are crude indicators that do not address institutional procedures, which case studies have examined and found important to student outcomes (Rosenbaum, Deil-Amen, and Person, 2006). More research is needed to examine the influences of such procedures on student success.

Recommendations

Current policy proposals often build on the assumption that institutions differ in their impact on student outcomes. If confirmed by subsequent research, these analyses suggest that federal, state, and institutional decision makers should consider basing policies on more stable empirical foundations. In particular, recommendations from this study follow.

1. The use of the institutional graduation rate as a proxy for institutional effectiveness should be treated with skepticism. According to these analyses, the institutional graduation rate provides no useful information for the highest- and lowest-achieving community college students, controlling for other institutional characteristics. Therefore, policymakers and practitioners seeking to foster success in different groups of stu-

dents, such as underprepared students, should develop and use different or more nuanced measures of institutional effectiveness.

2. Colleges are advised to explore existing data and methods similar to those described in this chapter to identify key institutional attributes likely to improve the success of particular groups of students. For example, increasing or decreasing involvement of part-time faculty, bolstering particular student services, or investing in different instructional practices can be assessed in terms of advantages and disadvantages for underprepared students.

3. These results raise concerns about whether community college students attending institutions with high proportions of minorities may be structurally shortchanged in ways that seriously harm students' degree completion. More research is needed to understand and improve student success dynamics at these institutions. For example, studies need to examine how students receive information and make decisions about delaying college, attending part-time, and interrupting or changing colleges because all of these choices have been shown to have strong harmful effects on completion (Bozick and Deluca, 2005; Goldrick-Rab, 2006; Hearn, 1992; Peter and Cataldi, 2005). Similarly, more research is needed to assess whether community colleges' graduation rates are determined, in part, by how many students enroll in majors with high completion rates because it is likely that individuals' completion rates are strongly related to the labor market payoffs they can anticipate for degree completion in their majors (Rosenbaum, Deil-Amen, and Person, 2006).

National policy discussions have focused narrowly on institutional graduation rate without considering how different institutional procedures and offerings may interact with students' academic preparation to affect later outcomes including earnings and occupations (Stephan and Rosenbaum, 2008). This poses a serious risk of pressuring colleges to exclude costly, high-risk students, while it provides no useful guidance about constructive actions that colleges can take to help different groups of students. This chapter provides an initial effort toward showing how research can inform such improvements.

References

Alexander, K., and Eckland, B. K. "Contextual Effects in the High School Attainment Process." *American Sociological Review,* 1975, *40*(3), 402–416.

Bailey, T., and others. *Community College Student Success: What Institutional Characteristics Make a Difference?* New York: Columbia University, Teachers College, Community College Research Center, 2005.

Bean, J. P. "Student Attrition, Intentions, and Confidence: Interaction Effects in a Path Model." *Research in Higher Education,* 1982, *17*(4), 291–320.

Bozick, R., and DeLuca, S. "Better Late Than Never? Delayed Enrollment in the High School to College Transition." *Social Forces,* 2005, *84*(1), 531–554.

Braxton, J. M., Hirschy, A. S., and McClendon, S. A. *Toward Understanding and Reducing College Student Departure.* ASHE-ERIC Higher Education Report 30, no. 3. San Francisco: Jossey-Bass, 2004.

Dougherty, K., and Hong, E. "Performance Accountability as Imperfect Panacea: The Community College Experience." In T. Bailey and V. Morest (eds.), *Defending the Community College Equity Agenda.* Baltimore, Md.: Johns Hopkins University Press, 2006.

Goldrick-Rab, S. "Following Their Every Move: How Social Class Shapes Postsecondary Pathways." *Sociology of Education,* 2006, 79(1), 61–79.

Hearn, J. C. "Determinants of Postsecondary Education Attendance: Some Implications of Alternative Specifications of Enrollment." *Educational Evaluation and Policy Analysis,* 1988, 10(2), 172–185.

Hearn, J. C. "Emerging Variations in Postsecondary Attendance Patterns: An Investigation of Part-Time, Delayed, and Nondegree Enrollment." *Research in Higher Education,* 1992, 33(6), 657–687.

Hoachlander, G., Sikora, A. C., and Horn, L. *Community College Students: Goals, Academic Preparation, and Outcomes.* Washington, D.C.: U.S. Department of Education, National Center for Education Statistics, 2003.

Pascarella, E. T., and Terenzini, P. T. *How College Affects Students: A Third Decade of Research.* San Francisco: Jossey-Bass, 2005.

Peter, K., and Cataldi, E. F. *The Road Less Traveled? Students Who Enroll in Multiple Institutions.* Washington, D.C.: U.S. Department of Education, National Center for Education Statistics, 2005.

Rosenbaum, J. E., Deil-Amen, R., and Person, A. *After Admission: From College Access to College Success.* New York: Russell Sage Foundation, 2006.

Sewell, W. H., and Shah, V. P. "Socioeconomic Status, Intelligence, and the Attainment of Higher Education." *Sociology of Education,* 1967, 40(1), 1–23.

StataCorp. *Stata Statistical Software: Release 9.* College Station, Tex.: StataCorp, 2005.

Stephan, J. L., and Rosenbaum, J. E. "The Impact of Choice of Major on Earnings by High School Achievement." Unpublished manuscript, Northwestern University, 2008.

Tinto, V. *Leaving College.* Chicago: University of Chicago Press, 1993.

Titus, M. "An Examination of the Influence of Institutional Context on Student Persistence at Four-Year Colleges and Universities: A Multilevel Approach." *Research in Higher Education,* 2004, 45(7), 673–697.

Wilson, W. J. *When Work Disappears: The World of the New Urban Poor.* New York: Random House, 1996.

LISBETH J. GOBLE *is a doctoral student in human development and social policy at Northwestern University in Evanston, Illinois.*

JAMES E. ROSENBAUM *is a professor of sociology, education, and social policy at Northwestern University in Evanston, Illinois.*

JENNIFER L. STEPHAN *is a doctoral student in human development and social policy at Northwestern University in Evanston, Illinois.*

7

This chapter explores the ways that information networks are related to student persistence in the community college and how institutional structures can encourage such networks.

Information Networks and Integration: Institutional Influences on Experiences and Persistence of Beginning Students

Melinda Mechur Karp, Katherine L. Hughes

Because they are conveniently located, open-access, and low-cost, community colleges tend to enroll students who are more socially, economically, and academically disadvantaged than do other postsecondary institutions. However, despite colleges' strong efforts and investment in an array of strategies intended to increase persistence and graduation rates, student success at community colleges remains low. In a recent study of community college enrollment, 45 percent of community college students had earned a certificate or degree or had transferred to a four-year institution within six years of their initial enrollment (Bailey, Jenkins, and Leinbach, 2005). While 8 percent of students were still enrolled, 47 percent had left school without earning a credential (Bailey and others, 2005).

This chapter uses data from a qualitative exploratory study at two urban community colleges to examine experiences of beginning students, paying close attention to the influence that institutional information networks have on students' perceptions and persistence. We find that students' reported integration, or sense of belonging in the institution, is positively associated with their persistence to a second year of enrollment. This sense of belonging is encouraged by students' involvement in information networks, a group of social ties that helped them understand college life. Moreover, we find that the institutional environment can encourage the creation of these networks through formal mechanisms such as Student Success courses. This

finding provides colleges with tools to encourage integration and, potentially, persistence. However, we also find that the same structures that promote information networks can serve as inadvertent stratifying mechanisms; colleges therefore need to be attendant to the ways that the institutional environment can discourage as well as encourage student success.

Methods and Data

We conducted a study of student persistence in community colleges to explore, among other things, how students report on their initial institutional experiences and the relationship between those experiences and progress toward a degree. We conducted interviews with community college students during their second semester of enrollment and re-interviewed the students six months later, whether they remained enrolled or not. Participants were students in two urban community colleges in the Northeast enrolling significant numbers of minority and economically disadvantaged students (we refer to these institutions by the pseudonyms, Northern CC and Eastern CC).

Students were randomly selected from a list of all first-time enrollees, both full and part time, in fall 2005 who persisted to spring 2006. Nonmatriculating and continuing education students, as well as those who already had earned a postsecondary degree elsewhere, were excluded. Letters of invitation to participate in the study were sent to 176 students; each potential participant was also contacted by telephone at least three times at various times of the day to secure their participation in the study. Participants were offered a cash stipend of one hundred dollars (fifty dollars per interview). Despite these efforts, we had a low take-up rate so we supplemented the sample using a snowball technique for recruitment of additional students.

Forty-four students were interviewed in the spring semester; the first row of Table 7.1 shows the demographic characteristics of this sample. We were able to reinterview thirty-six of these students in fall 2006; these responses, as well as responses by student demographics, are shown in the bottom three rows of Table 7.1.

During both waves of data collection, interviews lasted approximately sixty minutes and followed a semistructured interview protocol. All interviews were recorded and transcribed for analysis. The spring 2006 interviews focused on students' initial experiences in college, including their perception of and experiences in their courses; use and knowledge of student services, such as counseling and tutoring centers; and relationships with classmates and professors. We also asked what the college could do to make it easier for them to progress toward a degree. The fall 2006 interviews focused on students' decisions to continue in college or not and on the challenges they faced in progressing toward their degree goals. In particular, we probed for how their social and academic relationships, knowledge and use of the institutional services available, and sense of comfort on campus contributed to their progress toward a degree or lack thereof.

NEW DIRECTIONS FOR COMMUNITY COLLEGES • DOI: 10.1002/cc

Table 7.1. By School and Demographic Characteristics: First-Round Participants and Second-Round Responses

	College		Gender		Race				
	Eastern CC	Northern CC	Female	Male	Black	White	Hispanic	Asian/ Pacific Islander	Unknown
First round participants (N = 44)	25	19	28	16	11	14	10	7	2
Second round participants (N = 36)	21	15	22	14	8	13	8	6	1
Unable to schedule* (N = 5)	3	2	4	1	3	0	0	1	1
No response** (N = 3)	1	2	2	1	0	1	2	0	0

* Participants who did not show up for a scheduled interview, or students we spoke to but never scheduled a second interview with in fall 2006.

** Participants who never responded to repeated phone calls and flyer attempts to schedule the second interview in fall 2006.

The transcribed interviews were uploaded to Nvivo, a software program for analyzing qualitative data (QSR International, 2006). We created codes addressing student perceptions of their courses and the presence of various social relationships. We coded students for their reported sense of belonging in the institution and the types of social networks of which they were part. We also coded student attributes, including race, socioeconomic status, and gender, as well as student progress toward a degree.

Once the transcripts were coded, we read the interviews thematically, examining the ways that students discussed various aspects of their college environments. For example, we read all transcript pieces related to course experiences, as well as all transcript sections related to information networks. We sought themes that emerged from the data.

Integration and Information Networks

Theorists of higher education have posited that students who become integrated into college are more likely to persist toward a degree (Tinto, 1993). This theory of integration hypothesizes that students who feel connected to the social or academic activities of the college are more likely to feel comfortable there and so are less likely to leave the institution. Integration can be created in the classroom, through relationships with others, or through participation in extracurricular activities such as clubs or teams.

Although some have doubted this theory's applicability to community college students, given its focus on creating relationships outside of the classroom, our study found that community college students often do become integrated into the institution. We coded students as integrated if they reported feeling comfortable on the campus or reported enjoying their time in college or their classes during their first interview.

Thirty-one students, or 70 percent of the sample, reported feeling a sense of belonging on campus. Thirteen students did not report an attachment to the institution. Given Tinto's integration framework, we would expect that those students reporting a sense of belonging would be more likely to persist to their second year of enrollment. Of the 40 students whose enrollment status in the fall of 2006 was known to us, those who were coded as being integrated were more likely to persist. Nearly 90 percent of students who were integrated into the college persisted to the second year. Just over two-thirds of those who were not integrated did so. (It should be noted that our sample had an unusually high rate of persistence overall.)

Given these findings, we sought to understand the institutional contexts that promoted the creation of attachments to the community college. In analyzing the data thematically, we found that students' participation in information networks was an important mechanism in encouraging integration. We defined *information networks* as social ties that facilitated the transfer of institutional knowledge and procedures. In other words, knowing people to say hello to in the hallways did not strongly influence students' sense of belonging; knowing people through whom one could learn about professors, course options, or support services did. The information networks in which students participated could include either professors or classmates, but they had to be made of ties that were strong enough to promote information gathering.

Twenty-seven students in our sample (61 percent) reported engaging in an information network; seventeen students (38 percent) did not. Twenty-six of the thirty-one students who were coded as integrated into the college also reported being part of an information network (84 percent). One student of the thirteen who were not integrated was part of a network (8 percent). It appears, then, that having an information network is related to being integrated into the college. We cannot discern the direction of causality given the exploratory nature of the data. However, given student reports of the importance of information in encouraging a sense of belonging on campus, we assume that these networks facilitate integration, not the reverse.

Information networks helped make the campus feel more manageable and friendlier to students. These networks also helped them overcome obstacles so that they did not become alienated from or frustrated with the institution. As a result, these networks appear to help students feel at home on campus while giving them the tools to be successful there.

NEW DIRECTIONS FOR COMMUNITY COLLEGES • DOI: 10.1002/cc

Information networks achieved these benefits in a variety of ways. First, they helped students make connections throughout the campus. Because most students commute to campus, their college experience is often limited to the classroom. They come to class and then leave again. Thus, navigating the larger social space, learning about the resources available to them outside of the classroom, and feeling connected to a broader institution can be challenging.

Information networks help students overcome this. For example, students can learn about campus resources, such as tutoring or supplemental support programs, through networks of classmates. Moreover, students reported that learning about campus resources through social relationships, rather than through printed materials or other forms of information, helped them feel comfortable actually using the resource. Heidi (all student names are pseudonyms), a Northern CC student, was introduced to support services staff as part of an introductory Student Success course. She found it very helpful, saying, "But now you feel more comfortable; now you know the library and you know who to ask if you were looking for something." Due to their information networks, students' social connections began to extend beyond the confines of the classroom, and the social space of the institution became familiar and welcoming.

Second, students reported that the social nature of information networks made their time on campus more enjoyable. These networks gave students a reason beyond pure academics to want to come to school. To some extent, this is not surprising. However, it is interesting that students differentiated between superficial relationships with people they knew in passing and more meaningful ones predicated on information exchange. Debra from Eastern CC, for example, maintained that there was a difference between most of the people she knew in college and her one best friend, saying of the former, "I don't talk to them outside of class, only in class. I got some of their phone numbers just in case, but I don't use them." Her one good friend, on the other hand, helped her learn things about the college and made her feel comfortable there. "We go through the same experiences, the same feelings, of how we view school. We help each other on work." This friend also gave Debra advice on professors.

The relationships that made up information networks, therefore, were more significant to students and created stronger attachments to the institutions than those that did not serve to provide information. Knowing people on campus made academic life fun, but also meaningful. The ties between individuals in these networks were made stronger due to their use in facilitating information exchange and therefore held more sway over students.

Finally, information networks appear to facilitate students' access to good information and sources of support. This stood in contrast to the channels more typically used by community college students. For example, students often used information networks to get quality course advising. In both colleges, the typical way of receiving course advice was to meet with a general college counselor who did not have an ongoing relationship with the student or to use printed college materials such as a course catalogue. These methods often led to inadequate or inaccurate advice; they also left students feeling little connection to the college. Eddy (Northern CC) described the process as "throwing darts at a board."

Students who were part of information networks gained quality information about courses. Mike (Northern CC), for example, created relationships with faculty members in his department, which he used to gain information about required courses. He had multiple conversations about his goals and program of study, and found that this helped him feel comfortable in his course decisions. He said, "You get to know them, and you form a relationship with them and get in contact with them. And they like you and well, you feel like you have somebody in the system to help you out." In this way, Mike obtained information but also developed a sense that he belonged in the institution, and that people in the college cared about him and his future.

All three benefits of information networks—campus connections, social contact, and information and support—encourage students to feel connected to the college. Students who engage in information networks begin to believe that there are people at the college who want them to succeed and who will make sure that they attain their goals. Students who do not have these resources can feel adrift, as though nobody on campus cares about their future. They often expressed a belief that the college was set up to promote failure and felt frustrated with their institutional experiences. In contrast, students who were part of information networks found that they could navigate the college and felt that they could find ways to overcome challenges. They also felt attached to the college and thus were willing to continue with their education, even as some of them faced significant academic difficulty.

Institutional Environment and the Creation of Information Networks

Given their importance in encouraging integration, we asked how students develop information networks. In examining the interview data, we found that students generally reported developing these networks within the classroom. This means that institutions can structure their environments to help students create these beneficial relationships.

For many students, one particular facet of the institution strongly encouraged the creation of information networks and, in turn, integration. This was the Student Success course, also called "College Survival" or "College 101." Student Success courses are one-credit courses conceived of as a way to orient students to college, provide them with information about the college, and help them develop skills that will encourage their success in college.

Our data indicate that, in addition to orienting students to the college, the structure and content of the Student Success courses facilitate the development of information networks. These further encouraged integration into the college for participants. Leroy, a Northern CC student, described the resulting integration the most succinctly, saying that the course was the class that "got you into college." His use of the word "into" strongly indicated that he felt integrated, or attached, to the institution after taking the Student Success class.

Student Success courses encouraged the development of information networks in a number of ways. First, the content of the course exposed students to a variety of staff members and helped them identify individuals to include in their networks. This exposure was carried out through guest speakers as well as guided tours of a range of college offices, such as the tutoring center. These introductions helped students feel comfortable approaching these offices and gave them a touchstone when they were seeking help.

Second, the course included a variety of group projects and discussions that facilitated the development of peer networks. The focus of these networks was academic rather than peer culture. In most sections of the course, for example, students were graded on their participation, which pushed them to engage with other students. Eddy (Northern CC) described the Student Success course as encouraging students to "crack that shy shell." His comments suggested that the course was structured to encourage the creation of networks, saying, "[The instructor would] have us work more in groups . . . and you've got to talk to the person next to you, and we're all laughing; it was like, this isn't that bad. . . . I think that really helps."

Third, the course provided students with clear faculty member contacts to use as resources for guidance and support. Many students described the ways that they used their Student Success professors as their main resources for information and connectedness on campus. The structure of the Student Success course encouraged interactions between students and professors, so students felt that their Student Success professors knew them and their goals well. This enabled the Student Success course professors, who were frequently counselors, to give students individualized course advice, which was greatly appreciated. Because students had a relationship with and trusted their professors, they often sought them out after the class ended. Jasmine (Northern CC), for example, continued to meet with her Student Success professor long after the course ended, saying, "She's sort of like my go-to person now."

Institutions can structure student experiences to promote information networks outside of Student Success courses as well. One important way they can do this is by encouraging the use of student-centered pedagogies. Students reported that classes using these pedagogies helped them develop information networks and feel that they belonged on the campus. For example, many students highlighted the ways that classroom discussions helped them develop relationships that could be used to learn about the campus and become comfortable within it. Asha (Eastern CC) described class discussions by saying, "When you're having a group discussion you tend to interact invariably and that interaction leads to friendship." Carla, another Eastern CC student, expanded upon this by explaining the way that these friendships can lead to information: "Also, for knowing what good professors to take I rely on my classmates' opinions because a lot of them have been here longer than I have or they've had to repeat a class or something like that."

A Word of Caution: Structuring Stratification

Our qualitative research supports the notion that institutional environments can encourage student integration and persistence. In particular, structured environmental features such as Student Success courses can facilitate students' sense of belonging and trust in the institution. However, our data also provide a cautionary tale. As institutions create interventions aimed at increasing integration, they may also inadvertently create structures that reproduce inequality and stratification.

At Northern CC, only full-time students had to enroll in the Student Success course; part-time students were exempt. Students not required to take the course did not do so. For example, none of the part-time students from Northern CC in our sample enrolled in the class. One student, Daria, even asked if she should take the class and was discouraged from doing so, saying, "I asked if I had to take this class [Student Success], and they said no I don't have to because I'm a part-time student. I say what if I go back and be a full-time. [They said] you're not now, so you don't have to." Similarly, some students at Eastern CC found ways to get around the requirement to take the course, at least temporarily, and did not enroll in a Student Success course during their first semester in college.

Students who did not take the course were clearly disadvantaged in their academic pursuits, as illustrated by Tammy, a Northern CC student who did not receive tutoring assistance because she was not well informed about the tutoring program at her college. "Sometimes they have like tutors in the building, peers. But I've never been to one myself personally because usually they charge. But besides that I don't—I haven't really—there's nowhere else to really go to, like that for help." Tutoring at Northern CC was actually free, a fact that was discussed multiple times in the Student Success course.

The part-time students in our sample were more likely to have entered college with fewer resources than were their full-time peers. They were more likely to work full-time, thereby limiting both the social networks they were able to form on campus as well as the amount of time they could devote to exploring campus resources independently. These students also tended to be older, thus lacking family resources that could help them navigate college. In contrast, the full-time students in our sample were more likely to have families who supported their college educations, financially and otherwise. Those whose preexisting resources enabled them to attend college full time were better able to acquire the contacts with people and the information that could help them navigate the college environment. Ironically, then, those students most in need of institutional help in creating information networks and information in our study were the ones who were least likely to receive them.

Conclusions and Recommendations

We conducted an exploratory study of initial student experiences in two community colleges. We found that most students report feeling a sense of integration in their institutions and that this integration is related to persistence to a second semester. We also found that this integration appears to be facilitated by student involvement in information networks, defined as relationships that provide individuals with access to valuable information.

From the data, it appears that information networks are developed through, among other things, structured institutional activities like Student Success courses. These courses provide opportunities for students to connect and engage with peers and professors in meaningful ways and to develop relationships that allow them to have faith in the institution and feel that they belong in college. An important caution is needed, however; we also found that in some cases, institutional policies surrounding access to Student Success courses actually served as stratifying mechanisms. Students who most needed access to the Student Success course and the information networks it facilitates were the least likely to actually take the course, and thus were further disadvantaged.

The findings have implications for community college practice. First, colleges should find ways to help students develop information networks. These ways could include developing more classes like Student Success that help students learn about the college, perhaps by using the college as a laboratory or by expecting students to use college facilities. They also include encouraging and helping professors to develop student-centered pedagogies such as those used in Student Success courses to help students develop substantive relationships with one another.

Second, the findings remind colleges that they should think through the unintended consequences of their policies and ascertain that they promote, rather than inhibit, student participation in Student Success and similar courses. This includes ensuring that such courses are required of all students, not just some, and that students take these courses at the beginning of their college careers rather than later on.

Finally, the findings presented here remind us that institutional environments influence student experiences in college. These environments are not outside of college personnel's control; rather, they can be structured to benefit students. Creating formal structures that encourage information networks, which, in turn, foster integration, can increase the likelihood that students will remain enrolled in college and attain a degree.

References

Bailey, T., Jenkins, D., and Leinbach, T. *Is Student Success Labeled Educational Failure? Student Goals and Graduation Rates in the Accountability Debate at Community Colleges.* New York: Community College Research Center, Teachers College, Columbia University, 2005.

QSR International. *NVivo: Version 7.* Doncaster, Australia: QSR International, 2006.

Tinto, V. *Leaving College: Rethinking the Causes and Cures of Student Attrition.* (2nd ed.) Chicago: University of Chicago Press, 1993.

MELINDA MECHUR KARP *is a senior research associate at the Institute on Education and the Economy/Community College Research Center, Teachers College, Columbia University, in New York City.*

KATHERINE L. HUGHES *is assistant director for work and education reform research at the Institute on Education and the Economy/Community College Research Center, Teachers College, Columbia University, in New York City.*

8

This chapter describes the evolution and implementation of the California Basic Skills Initiative, one of the most sweeping initiatives to address the needs of students in California community college history.

The California Basic Skills Initiative

Barbara Illowsky

The California Community Colleges (CCC) system forms the largest system of higher education in the world; in the 2006–2007 academic year it served more than 2.6 million students (California Community College Chancellor's Office, 2008). The system is central to maintaining the social and economic health of the state through its certificates, degrees, workforce programs, and transfer pathways. Perhaps even more critical, community colleges open the doors of higher education to all, providing significantly more postsecondary course work than any other higher education segment in the state.

Assisting the underprepared student to attain the basic skills needed to succeed in college-level work has been a core function of community colleges throughout their history. This is a major challenge: 70 to 80 percent of first-time college students in the CCC need work in developmental mathematics, English as a second language (ESL), writing, or reading courses. In 2006–2007, 700,000 students were enrolled in these below-college-level courses (California Community College Chancellor's Office, 2008).

To date, efforts to address the needs of students requiring basic skills have met with varying levels of success. Over the past seven years, basic skills course success rates have remained around 69 percent for ESL, 60 percent for English, and 54 percent for mathematics. Furthermore, only 29 percent of the students who enrolled in a basic skills class in the 2001–2002 academic year earned an associate's degree or vocational certificate or transferred to a four-year institution by 2006–2007 (California Community College Chancellor's Office, 2008). The significance of this low percentage is the concern that California's skilled workforce will soon be too small to serve the state's needs.

NEW DIRECTIONS FOR COMMUNITY COLLEGES, no. 144, Winter 2008 © 2008 Wiley Periodicals, Inc.
Published online in Wiley InterScience (www.interscience.wiley.com) • DOI: 10.1002/cc.348

There are several exemplary basic skills programs in the CCC; however, many of them are small in scale and relatively transient because they are funded through short-term grants. This chapter describes the evolution and implementation of the California Basic Skills Initiative (CA BSI), a statewide effort to address ongoing basic skills and ESL needs of community college students and of all campus faculty, administrators, and staff who support these students. CA BSI strategies include assisting every college in assessing its own successes and challenges, building upon those successes, and developing internal strategies to address the challenges. The ultimate goals of the CA BSI are to increase student retention and success, as well as to increase the knowledge of what supports those successes.

Definition of Terms

The following are working definitions of key terms developed as part of a literature review for the CA BSI:

- *Basic skills.* "Basic skills are those foundation skills in reading, writing, mathematics, and English as a Second Language, as well as learning skills and study skills, which are necessary for students to succeed in college-level work" (Academic Senate for California Community Colleges, 2007, p. 4). The specific inclusion of ESL in this definition recognizes that all ESL is not, by definition, subsumed under basic skills. Instead, ESL skills are considered as basic to the extent that a student is unable to succeed in college-level course work due to inability to speak, read, write, or comprehend English.
- *Effective practices.* Adapted from Boylan (2002), effective practices "refer to organization, administrative, instructional, or support activities engaged in by highly successful programs, as validated by research and literature sources relating to developmental education" (Academic Senate for California Community Colleges, 2007, p. 4).

Evolution of Basic Skills Initiative

Three events over the past several years led to the development and funding of the CA BSI. First, the CCC Board of Governors (BOG) adopted a comprehensive new strategic plan in 2006 to strengthen student success and readiness (California Community Colleges System Office, 2006). The CA BSI is a key component of this goal.

Second, the BOG approved the raising of the statewide minimum English and mathematics graduation requirements for all students earning associate of art or associate of science degrees. Effective fall 2009, all entering students who earn associate's degrees must demonstrate proficiency in freshman English composition and competence in mathematics at the level of intermediate algebra. Leading up to the BOG's unanimous decision was what has been described as unprecedented cooperation among the Academic Senate for CCC, state instructional officers, and state student services officers. The presidents of these organizations, Ian Walton, Pam Deegan, and Robin Richards, jointly developed the idea of the CA BSI. The chancellor's office then embraced the idea and provided funding for it. That funding was the third major event in the evolution of the initiative.

To date, implementation of the CA BSI has occurred in three phases: widespread dissemination of information on effective practices, professional development to allow colleges to examine their basic skills and ESL efforts and determine how to improve them, and funding to allow colleges to act on the first two. In each phase, the majority of the funds went to the individual colleges to assist them in implementing their action plans with remaining funds to provide professional development opportunities statewide as described later in this chapter.

Widespread Dissemination of Information

The first phase of the CA BSI was led by Robert Gabriner of the Research and Planning Group and produced a document containing three parts: a review of literature and effective practices, an assessment tool for effective practices in basic skills, and a tool to estimate costs and downstream revenue.

Literature Review. The research group developed an extensive literature review related to basic skills practices, as well as an overview of examples of strategies employed by thirty-three community colleges and nine out-of-state institutions; it references over 250 sources, making this study the most comprehensive basic skills study conducted in CCC to date (California Community College Chancellor's Office, 2008). Researchers identified a consistent set of elements that characterize effective programs. An important criterion for inclusion was published program data that demonstrate success. The literature review outlines twenty-six practices in the four major categories:

1. *Organizational and administrative practices.* Institutional choices concerning structure, organization, and management have been related to the overall effectiveness of developmental education programs. Effective practices identified in this area include ensuring that developmental education is a clearly stated institutional priority. In addition, the developmental education program should be centralized or highly coordinated. In addition, institutional policies should facilitate student completion of necessary developmental course work as early as possible in the educational sequence and a comprehensive system of support services should be developed. The last two effective practices in the organizational and administrative strand include hiring faculty who are both knowledgeable and enthusiastic about developmental education and managing faculty and student expectations regarding developmental education.

2. *Program components.* According to the literature, a number of specific programmatic components are characteristic of highly effective

NEW DIRECTIONS FOR COMMUNITY COLLEGES • DOI: 10.1002/cc

developmental education programs. The literature review identified four specific effective practices in this strand. First, orientation, assessment, and placement are mandatory for all new students. Next, regular program evaluations are conducted, results are disseminated widely, and data are used to improve practice. Additionally, counseling support is provided with academic courses or programs. Finally, financial aid is disseminated to support developmental students. Mechanisms exist to ensure that developmental students are aware of such opportunities and are provided with assistance to apply for and acquire financial aid.

3. *Staff development.* According to the literature, the importance of comprehensive training and development opportunities for faculty and staff who work with developmental students cannot be underestimated. Programs with a strong professional development component have been shown to yield better student retention rates and better student performance in developmental courses than those without such an emphasis. Specific training is one of the leading variables contributing to the success of a variety of components of developmental instruction, including tutoring, advising, and instruction. The literature suggests that administrators should support and encourage faculty development in basic skills, and the improvement of teaching and learning is connected to the institutional mission. Next, the faculty should play a primary role in needs assessment, planning, and implementation of staff development programs and activities in support of basic skills programs. In addition, staff development programs need to be structured and appropriately supported to sustain them as ongoing efforts related to institutional goals for the improvement of teaching and learning. The last two effective practices in staff development are that staff development opportunities are flexible, varied, and responsive to developmental needs of individual faculty, diverse student populations, and coordinated programs and that faculty development is clearly connected to intrinsic and extrinsic faculty reward structures.

4. *Instructional practices.* Effective instructional practices are the key to achieving desired student outcomes for developmental programs. Research has linked the following instructional practices with success for developmental learners. The first of these practices is applying sound principles of learning theory to the design and delivery of courses in the developmental program. Additionally, curricula and practices that have proven to be effective within specific disciplines are employed. The developmental education program should also address holistic development of all aspects of the student. Attention is paid to the social and emotional development of the students as well as to their cognitive growth. Next, culturally responsive teaching theory and practices are applied to all aspects of the developmental instructional programs and services. In addition, a high degree of structure is provided in developmental education courses. Developmental education faculty employ a variety of instructional methods to accommodate student

diversity, and programs align entry and exit skills among levels and link course content to college-level performance requirements. Finally, developmental education faculty should routinely share instructional strategies and monitor student performance (Academic Senate for California Community Colleges, 2007).

Self-Assessment Tool. The self-assessment tool is a series of templates and questions to assist colleges in determining their strengths and weaknesses in basic skills education. The tool is directly linked to the findings of the literature review. It is designed to engage college administrators, faculty, and staff in a meaningful and reflective dialogue about their current practices and plans for program improvement, enhancement, or modification. The tool is organized around the four major areas and twenty-six effective practices. The tool also contains a variety of suggested strategies for accomplishing each practice as well as a series of prompts that will assist institutions with evaluating their current progress in each effective practice. A matrix is included for each section to allow colleges to develop a plan for changes, enhancements, or modifications. The purpose of the self-assessment tool is to allow colleges to determine how their current practices fit with and reflect the effective practices for basic skills cited in the literature.

Cost-Revenue Model. The cost-revenue model, developed by researchers Robert Johnstone and Jim Fillpot, provides a way to explore the incremental revenues that can be derived over time from effective basic skills programs, practices, or interventions. Interventions or programs targeting underprepared students at the community college are characterized by their limited scope and concerns for their expense. The literature review outlines the paths toward a fundamental change in basic skills instruction. The cost-revenue model explores how this change can be fiscally responsible. In many cases, the research indicates that these programs may pay for themselves or even result in a net benefit. The goal of this section is to provide a different way of thinking about the cost of these alternate developmental education programs.

Statewide Professional Development

I led a steering committee of California community college stakeholders that advised the work of the second and third phases. The Foothill-De Anza Community College District and the Academic Senate for California Community Colleges collaborated to develop and implement the grant activities. The second phase took place from February through December 2007, engaging administrators and faculty across disciplines and in student services in discussions about how to assess their current practices and how to create an action plan at their respective colleges.

Workshops and Conferences. Joint faculty- and administrative-led teams conducted twenty day-long regional workshops from May through

October for all California community college districts in the area of developmental education. The training was based on all three sections of *Basic Skills as a Foundation for Student Success in the California Community Colleges*. Approximately 1,600 faculty, administrators, and staff from colleges and continuing education centers in the CCC system participated in the training meetings. In addition, steering committee members presented papers to inform over 1,500 other California community college faculty, administrators, staff, and students at their annual professional conferences.

Evaluations of Workshops. After all the regional meetings were completed, all attendees were sent a final evaluation. One-eighth of the total participants, representing a cross-section of faculty, administrators, and researchers, as well as most of the colleges responded. Of these people, 88.2 percent said yes to the question, "Looking back at the regional meetings, did they help you understand basic skills effective practices?" Of the no responses, most listed that they had already read and studied the literature. Over 80 percent responded yes to the question, "Did the regional meetings help you prepare for developing your action plan?" Further details about assistance on institutional action plans will be addressed in the Phase III discussion.

Self-Assessment Tools. Another Phase II activity was to provide guidance to colleges as they completed their self-assessment, using the online templates described previously. The Self-Assessment Tool was piloted at twelve colleges in the spring and summer of 2007. The process results, along with tips, reports, and final reporting matrices, were posted on the Basic Skills Initiative (BSI) Web site (http://www.cccbsi.org) to provide additional assistance to all colleges, especially the smaller ones that did not have full-time institutional researchers. Follow-up in-person technical assistance was provided for the several colleges that requested it. The posted materials have been a valuable resource to other colleges in getting their own BSI committees organized and proceeding on track.

Brochure. Finally, the Steering Committee and RP Group produced a brochure highlighting and explaining the Basic Skills Initiative (Academic Senate for California Community Colleges, 2007). Copies of these brochures were distributed to the governor's office, the legislature, and all California community colleges and continue to be distributed at conferences.

Broadening Statewide Professional Development

Phase III of the Basic Skills Initiative runs from January through December 2008. This phase broadened the activities and obligations of statewide professional development as detailed below. At press, some of the activities described below have been completed and other programs are concurrently under way. On the individual campuses, colleges are implementing action plans based upon what they learned from conducting their self-assessment.

Literature Review. A follow-up to *Basic Skills as a Foundation for Success in California Community Colleges* is under way. This literature review focuses on three main areas: equity and diversity challenges and strategies, high school to college transition, and non-credit to credit transition. The document includes research that is backed by quantitative data, as well as strategies that seem promising, but need more time to produce representative data. A fourth section will be added in late 2008 on contextualized learning with basic skills embedded into occupational education courses and programs.

Regional Meetings and Summer Institute. In May and June 2008, faculty and administrators from all California community colleges were once again offered regional meetings. These free two-day meetings focused on integrating student services and counseling into the basic skills courses and programs. Program coordinators showcased their programs, strategies, and projects and worked with attendees on how to replicate these successful activities at their colleges. Outcomes assessment tools, including student learning outcomes and rubrics, were developed for basic skills students and faculty and for development of benchmarks in project and professional development. Attendees in the regional meetings actively participated in using these tools while examining their own basic skills success rates. The target audience for the regional meetings was vice presidents of instruction and of student services, counselors, student services staff, institutional researchers, coordinators of basic skills and student learning outcomes, and department chairs from writing, ESL, reading, mathematics, and occupational education departments.

Whereas the regional meetings target the leaders on campuses who can make programs happen, the summer institute is for the faculty in the classroom who work with students at the basic skills levels. In California, these include approximately fifty-eight thousand faculty, over half of them adjunct faculty. Many adjunct faculty are given the name "freeway flyers" as they travel from campus to campus trying to earn a living salary and rarely attend professional development activities or receive pedagogy mentoring. The summer institute is a four-day, completely free (including lodging, travel, and food) conference for adjunct faculty. It will focus on pedagogy and assessment for working with students at the basic skills level in both credit and non-credit courses. The attendees will be from reading, writing, ESL, mathematics, and occupational programs.

Database. Data collection of effective practices, strategies, and programs is currently under way. The database will be openly housed on the California Community Colleges Chancellor's Office Web site. It will contain both in- and out-of-state submissions. People will be able to search by any of the effective practices from the 2007 literature review. They will also be able to search by key words, targeted population, and college demographics. Each community college is expected to submit at least one entry. Many foundation-funded programs have already completed submissions. The database will be a living project. There are many extremely successful activities taking place all around the country. However, finding them is quite difficult. One goal is to include national submissions as well as those from California.

Workshops-to-Order and Online Professional Development. Colleges may make requests to the BSI Steering Committee training for specific needs to be held on their campuses. Teams of faculty and administrators will customize versions of the regional meetings and take them directly to the campuses. These workshops-to-order are open to all California community colleges. Thus far, requests for them have come from rural campuses that often do not have funding to send faculty and staff hundreds of miles to attend professional development seminars.

In view of the fact that the Summer Institute can only accommodate a few hundred of the over thirty thousand adjunct faculty in California, Phase III members will develop an online professional development site. The Web site will include videos of appropriate pedagogy in action, lesson plans for developmental students, and resources for further training.

Student Equity Plans. In 2005, all 109 California community colleges submitted Student Equity Plans to the California Community Colleges Chancellor's Office. At many colleges, these plans are shaping strategic plans and campus activities. At other colleges, especially those with recent senior leadership changes, the Student Equity Plans are long forgotten. A team of equity specialists from the colleges is working with the Chancellor's Office to review all 109 plans. They are aggregating statewide data for ESL and basic skills completion rates. They are disaggregating data by ethnicity and identifying areas of impact on overall and specific student populations. Success in basic skills is fundamental to educational equity. The team will help identify and promote statewide and specific individual college strategies. They are also assisting the colleges in developing their baseline data and benchmarks for increased ESL and basic skills student success.

Coordination. The Intersegmental Committee of Academic Senates (ICAS) is comprised of representatives from the academic senates of California Community Colleges, California State Universities, and Universities of California. In Phase III, mathematics faculty are working to review and revise as necessary the mathematics competency statements of what is expected in mathematics of entering college students. This document was last updated over a decade ago. The English competency statements were recently updated. Both updated documents will be shared in a broad forum in this phase.

Phase III team members will also collaborate with the Statewide Career Pathways project and Cal-PASS to form discussion groups in the areas of mathematics and English writing in the hopes of creating a common understanding of those competencies that students need to transition from high school to the college level.

Both internal and external communication to the California community colleges about the Basic Skills Initiative is one more aspect to Phase III. The Academic Senate for California Community Colleges will continue to sustain the Basic Skills Initiative Web site even after the grants are completed. Teams are developing newsletters and listservs and are investigating the use of blogs.

NEW DIRECTIONS FOR COMMUNITY COLLEGES • DOI: 10.1002/cc

Conclusion

The California Basic Skills Initiative is a key project in addressing the goal of student success and readiness in the CCC system strategic plan. The strategic plan emphasizes the community colleges' central role in meeting the state's social and economic needs. To succeed, the system must be significantly transformed in terms of how the colleges address and meet the needs of students with basic skills and ESL needs. Eliminating differential success rates within basic skills individual courses and in programs is a key component of educational equity. The requirements to effect organizational change are being met through a close collaboration of the Academic Senate for California Community Colleges, chief instructional officers, chief student services officers, chief executive officers, and the California Community Colleges Chancellor's Office. In the process, all major groups have clearly articulated why the colleges need to take steps to improve basic skills and ESL and why they need to move forward without delay.

Similar collaborations among constituencies on individual college campuses are fostering renewed energy and commitment to meeting the challenges of improving student learning in basic skills and ESL and extending the use of effective practices to the full range of college programs and services. Just as important, through this initiative, faculty, administrators, and Chancellor's Office personnel are working together respectfully as colleagues with the same goals. The level of interest that this project and the related statewide and local initiatives have already generated clearly suggests that California community colleges are beginning a new chapter in their efforts to provide a major pathway to higher education for all students.

References

Academic Senate for California Community Colleges. *Basic Skills as a Foundation for Student Success in California Community Colleges.* Sacramento: Academic Senate for California Community Colleges, 2007.

Boylan, H. *What Works: Research-Based Best Practices in Developmental Education.* Boone, N.C.: Continuous Quality Improvement Network and the National Center for Developmental Education, 2002.

California Community College Chancellor's Office. *Report on the System's Current Programs in English as a Second Language (ESL) and Basic Skills.* Sacramento: California Community College Chancellor's Office, 2008.

California Community Colleges System Office. *California Community Colleges System Strategic Plan.* Sacramento: California Community Colleges System Office, 2006.

BARBARA ILLOWSKY *is professor of mathematics at De Anza College in Cupertino, California, and project director for the California Basic Skills Initiative.*

9

Practitioners at individual community colleges and in-state agencies recognize the struggles of disadvantaged students, yet their combined efforts do not overcome the policies and practices that are contrary to advancing and aiding large student populations.

Institutional Efforts to Address Disadvantaged Students: An "Up-So-Down" View

John S. Levin

Community colleges have both sustained their rhetorical commitment to underserved populations and responded within the bounds of their limited resources to these populations. Nonetheless, practices of institutions have ignored some student needs, led to diminished responses to some needs, addressed a small portion of the population, and elevated a category of student behaviors (for example, program completion, university transfer, and job attainment) beyond other categories (for example, skill and personal development, social development and citizenship, and self-worth). Yet large numbers of faculty, staff, and administrators at colleges act deliberately to minister to the needs of disadvantaged students.

Disadvantaged students are those who by birth or circumstances (such as illness, plant closure, domestic strife, and the like) have barriers that either prevent or constrain their acquisition of basic rights and duties (Rawls, 1993). Barriers include financial discrimination against undocumented immigrants who are required to pay out-of-state tuition for college, which can be as much as five times that of in-state tuition, leading to either severe financial hardships or simply nonattendance. They also include high school experiences that resulted in noncompletion of a course of study that both credentialed students and supplied them with academic skills to cope with either the labor market or further education. Additionally, these barriers encompass abusive relationships in which children or adult women are

NEW DIRECTIONS FOR COMMUNITY COLLEGES, no. 144, Winter 2008 © 2008 Wiley Periodicals, Inc.
Published online in Wiley InterScience (www.interscience.wiley.com) • DOI: 10.1002/cc.349

removed or remove themselves from the home and face economic hardships. Finally, these obstacles include state and federal governments' unwillingness to provide financial support to colleges so that college costs are not passed on to students, costs which either constrain students' educational behaviors (for example, forcing them to work instead of taking classes and studying) or limit access.

The reasons for students participating in postsecondary education are multidimensional ranging from costs and time availability to self-perceptions and personal histories, as well as their physical, psychological, and mental states (Bowl, 2003; Silva, Cahalan, Lacireno-Paquet, and Mathematica Policy Research, 1998). This is especially the case for adult students (those twenty-five years and older) as well as for students from disadvantaged backgrounds. These students draw on different experiences such as immigrant backgrounds and base their decisions and choice making on their social and domestic conditions.

For example, O, a female student from Nigeria, has lived in the Chicago area for eight years, attends Truman College to gain English language skills, and has a goal of beginning a business. However, her family is fragmented and three of her children live in Nigeria, her educational background is limited, and English is not her primary language. O is not a student attempting to fit into dormitory life, a sorority, or even the freshman year experience. Her "life world" (Holland, Lachicotte, Skinner, and Cain, 1998) and her social world are not college. Even for those nontraditional students who are highly dependent upon college for their present sense of place and personal identity, such as the special education students at Johnston Community College in Smithfield, North Carolina, or the disabled students at Bakersfield College in Bakersfield, California, who participate in a college course called Tools for College Survival, college is only one factor in their "life world" and in their choices about their future circumstances.

The Problem of Disadvantaged Students

The purpose of educational institutions in a just society is to improve the position of these students in the acquisition of basic rights and duties (Rawls, 1993). Improvement signifies that institutions have advantaged students. The problem, however, is that increasingly our higher education institutions are adopting neo-liberal policies that favor privileged populations (Slaughter and Rhoades, 2004).

Personal benefits are slow to come to those who have been disadvantaged within their lifetimes and to those connected to groups who have been disadvantaged historically over generations. The flourishing of individuals is more likely for some populations than for others. Although access to education and to the acquisition of its benefits, such as economic and social mobility, appears to be part of both the distribution and gaining of advantage, specific student populations do not gain as much as others through this advantaging. The difference between access to a remedial program and to a university transfer program can be considerable, as can the difference between access to a community college and to a selective liberal arts college. Is the difference based upon social and economic inequalities? Did the institution address these inequalities during a student's educational career? Was there fair and reasonable distribution of resources to advantage disadvantaged students?

Our institutions and state systems of higher education make choices and indeed discriminate in their treatment of students, privileging some student populations over others. Students with disabilities, students who are in programs that have low institutional prestige such as developmental education, and students who are not legal immigrants to the United States may be treated differently than other students. Government policies also discriminate: the welfare population of single parents has constraints placed upon them as students that are not imposed upon other students (Shaw, Goldrick-Rab, Mazzeo, and Jacobs, 2005), and large numbers of part-time students are not qualified for financial aid.

For the broad student population, community colleges fail to advantage the disadvantaged; indeed, they disadvantage some student populations further. Community colleges and governments function in contrary ways. First, they fail to live up to the expectations for the community college as a responsive and democratic institution. Second, institutional and agency officials act against policies, both institutional and governmental, to respond to disadvantaged student populations. That is, institutional agents ignore or violate policies to serve students.

In what follows, an empirical investigation is briefly outlined and the complex issue of social mobility frames the discussion of community college strategies and behaviors directed to address student inequalities and disadvantaged conditions. In this context, behaviors of institutional agents, who are referred to as "squires," are not necessarily consistent with formal policy. The discussion concludes by articulating avenues to remedy parts of the problem for disadvantaged students.

The Study

This discussion is based upon a large field study that began in 2002 and involved thirteen community colleges in nine states. Data collection included interviews, document analysis, and on-site observations. Data were analyzed using the analytical framework of justice (Rawls, 1999) to understand both institutional practices accorded to adult and disadvantaged students and the behaviors of college and government officials. For further information on the study, see Levin (2007).

The community college has increasingly addressed student outcomes, including further education, employment, and learning. These outcomes serve as markers of student mobility, economically as well as socially, and reflect the community college's position as part of what scholars view as its place in the educational social structure (Cohen and Brawer, 2003; Frye, 1994; Labaree, 1997). Simultaneously, and largely consistent with state funding based upon student enrollments, community colleges have focused upon the recruitment and retention of students. Indeed, retention of students—their continuation beyond one course or one semester or one year of enrollment—has become a major concern of the institution, guiding institutional strategies that frame understandings of students, and particularly nontraditional students.

Although strategies of the institution are oriented toward student retention as well as student performance—strategies that have become synonymous with institutional goals—behaviors are less organized around principles and initiatives. A substantial portion of these individual behaviors is aimed at student mobility, such as access to the institution, movement of students through courses and programs, and movement beyond the institution to further education and employment. These patterns of progression can be viewed as well as social mobility, but that view might understate the effects of college upon disadvantaged students.

Is It All About Social Mobility?

One of the major arguments in higher education over the past five decades, an argument specifically focusing upon the community college, concerns the social mobility effects of college upon students. Although the promise of community colleges has centered upon individual advancement both economically and socially (Frye, 1994), scholars from Burton Clark (1960) to Kevin Dougherty (1994) have challenged the claim. In the past decade, the challenges have withered, yet the issue is pertinent for two reasons: first, because practitioners continue to make the claim that the community college advances the prospects of students, and second, because without social mobility for students who are disadvantaged, the institution serves as a place of containment for a large segment of the population.

My investigations indicate that the answer to the question of social mobility for disadvantaged students is mixed, complex, and nuanced when the views of community college practitioners are examined on this question. Even the president of Edmonds Community College (Edmonds, Washington), an ardent supporter of community college education for students, indicates that the issue of social mobility is muddied by the problem of resources because his college is not receiving enough revenue from the state to support student education. Yet, without the community college, the reverse of social mobility—a process or condition of social degradation—is the likely outcome for large populations. He notes:

> You're shooting yourself in the foot by serving all these people if you're not getting paid for them. But if we don't let them in, where are they going to go? . . . Well, they're going to go to jail; they're going to go on social [welfare] rolls; they're going to go to the local bar. They're sure not going to be contributing to society.

To the question, "Does the community college contribute to student social mobility?" college administrators and faculty responded in the affirmative, although their views contained mixed messages and their concept of mobility was more often than not economic. Indeed, several of the administrators and faculty viewed their college as a pipeline to employment. Indeed, the role of employment and employers has considerable salience in the community college, especially in those units of continuing education and contract training. In these program areas, student mobility may be dependent upon employers' views of the benefits of college education. In fields such as nursing, mobility is seen in economic terms, and the associate's credential in nursing has considerable appeal in the labor market. Yet wages are not the whole story for economic mobility: economic self-sufficiency leads to social benefits and the release of personal potential in the realm of individual accomplishment, as this member of the nursing faculty at Bakersfield College notes:

> I think that it adds to the overall self-esteem that they are self-supportive. Some people, unfortunately, come to nursing school so that they can be self-supportive so they can divorce and not have to be dependent on someone else. Some come back for the opposite reason: they got a divorce and they had no way to support themselves. So, there is that contribution that I think you see to society. . . . because of your earning power and what you can now do, and you never thought this was possible and the accomplishment that happens and occurs by being successful.

Others view the mobility issue as, on the one hand, fitting into the mainstream of American society, and on the other hand, as personal development and advancement. Personal enrichment and development are particularly evident in those students who have come to the community college from disadvantaged backgrounds: for example, those who are second language speakers of English. An ESL faculty member has this to say:

> I think in every aspect of their lives: communication, security, finding a job if they don't have one. Many of them get promoted. It's very exciting when they come back and tell you "Teacher, thank you. I learned more English. I got more money." . . . [There is] more involvement with their children in the schools, which is neat also because they get comfortable enough to be able to attend PTA and the programs their kids are in, talk to the teacher and different things: helping their families, that's a big one; learn English, work here; send money home; bring families here.

The answer to the question of social mobility for community college students is not a straightforward one. On one level, the acquisition of skills and knowledge is going to enhance a student's employment opportunities and social awareness, as a dean at the Community College of Denver notes: "Any time a student can get more education and improve their worldview and their earning power they win. They benefit." On another level, the outcomes of community college education, even the outcomes after the gaining of skills and knowledge, are limiting. "We are sometimes too reactive to the business community and build programs to fill a pipeline and put people into jobs that maybe they didn't want, weren't interested in, or that are dead end" notes this same dean. The social mobility issue is especially evident when students who are not advantaged, who lack appropriate academic backgrounds for college, or who are not native English language speakers are the object of an institution's goals to train students, as noted by a dean at Harry Truman College in Chicago, Illinois. "Our objective is to try to get them into a track to find a job and succeed and get a better paying job, besides being a waiter, or a bus boy, or a dishwasher."

Notwithstanding the considerable benefits that accrue to students through college attendance (Pascarella and Terenzini, 2005), for the institution called the community college it may not be a question so much as do students achieve social mobility as a question of does the institution adjust social and economic inequalities for its students?

Institutional Strategies and Actions

Strategies and actions within colleges focus on assisting students to access the institution and its programs, supporting students in their courses and programs, improving student academic performance, enhancing student experiences, and retaining students at the college or facilitating their movement to further education or employment. In the developmental learning program area, the use of learning communities for remedial education at Bakersfield College has proved to be one of the more successful approaches for underprepared students, who are predominantly Latino, with African Americans as the second most populous group in the program area.

Other strategies for nontraditional students include specific programs for subpopulations such as first-generation programs for students who are the first in their families to attend postsecondary education. Such programs also include adult high school programs for students who want to complete a high school diploma on a college campus or who attend a high school at a college campus and take college level courses either concurrently with or subsequent to their high school courses. First-generation programs, using federal funding, target populations that are merely samples of the larger first-generation population on campus. They serve as programs that advantage students by giving them not only services such as tutoring, but also privileges such as course registration priority. Of particular importance is the role these programs play in student persistence. Stacey, a thirty-year-old university transfer student in Early Childhood Education at the Community College of Denver (CCD; Denver, Colorado), typifies a first-generation student in one of these programs: "Right now I'm in the first generation program that's really helped me figure out where I'm going to go with my college career. . . . Without this program I think I'd be pretty lost with college." Without these strategies, program establishment, and the pursuit of funding by these institutions, Stacey and other similar students would be bypassed.

Institutional strategies can be more global, not merely single or limited programs or services, but based on traditions, past practices, and institutional culture, as evident at CCD, where a rational system of intervention pervades the institution. The CCD president says:

> I think the tradition at CCD has always been to examine how we are doing as an institution and how students are doing. . . . Students don't see . . . whoever is available; they have assigned advisors the entire time. . . . This case manager's job is to make sure that the student knows . . . about all the services.

Indeed, the president—and she asserts that this is a common institutional perception—does not view students in categories found in the trait framework, which suggests a deficiency model of students:

> The way I think about them, and I think that is true of CCD . . . is that they're not "at-risk." I think a lot of people [in other institutions] think of students like this, well you know, "these are difficult." I think, "No, this is who our market is; these are the students we serve, and they have a lot that we can learn from them about their life experiences."

The Community College of Denver grounds institutional strategy on broad categories of student needs, framing these needs in assumptions about student characteristics, which include ethnicity, economic status, and gender. The goals of strategies such as first-generation programs are to combine student access (participation in postsecondary education) with student attainment (course completion, program completion, and the movement to further either education or employment).

Institutional Behaviors

Institutional behaviors are a conglomerate of individual actions directed at students that are not necessarily consistent with strategy. They can be carried out by college faculty and administrators with personal agendas—that is, with motives that reflect the individual actor's values. These behaviors can have positive effects upon students as well as outcomes. Some of these behaviors are focused specifically on the most disadvantaged students.

NEW DIRECTIONS FOR COMMUNITY COLLEGES • DOI: 10.1002/cc

At Edmonds Community College, the program director responsible for the Work First program, which serves welfare recipients, positions herself as a "gateway" for the economically disadvantaged. The treatment of students for this program director is both at the individual level, addressing motivation and skill development, and at the group level for a population with lower abilities than the norm. She sees her program as serving not just welfare mothers, but also their children. Her descriptions of both her work and goals suggest that from this perspective, Edmonds Community College is a human services organization (Hasenfeld, 1983) attending to the needs of its service population, one that is particularly stressed. Yet, because of federal policy and regulations, her program cannot respond to those without children: men are excluded unless they are legal custodians of children, as are women without children. She describes her work and that of her colleagues as a rescue mission. She is not operating alone in her rescue mission, but as part of a group of like-minded faculty at her college.

Individual behaviors of institutional members also often cross the line of institutional legitimacy or policy. At Bakersfield College, a program administrator serves as a gateway for underserved populations as he works the system for students. The director of the cooperative education department says:

> The job of that . . . program is to place students with disabilities in jobs. In other words, take them through their job search to assist them, and that is a very, very difficult thing to do. . . . So, I took over that program and put . . . two programs together . . . what they called these summer youth employment training program[s], where they offered grants to higher education to work with individuals from ages fourteen to twenty-one over the summer. So, I took over that program . . . but what I did was change it. I limited the students to age seventeen, graduating seniors, because I also made it mandatory for them to do an internship. So, I turned it into a job, into an internship, and paid them to go to school, bought their books and everything. . . . Then we moved from an early childhood education literacy program, combining with that a fostered youth mentoring program, then a tutorial assistance grant, and now we have a smart team out on disabled. I went from just one program to almost four and I wanted to do more, but they are not going to let me do it.

This midlevel administrator altered the formal structure of college programs to fit the perceived needs of minority students, most of whom were Latino. In educating these students, he was, in his words, performing community social service. With an almost insatiable appetite for establishing and administering programs to eradicate educational impoverishment, this college administrator operated his own educational system even though his main responsibility was cooperative education. The extent to which college and college system officials operate individually, sometimes beyond formal policy, is nearly endemic within the thirteen institutions addressed in my research.

NEW DIRECTIONS FOR COMMUNITY COLLEGES • DOI: 10.1002/cc

Institutional Squires

Among the many behaviors, including those of college officials and system and state policy actors, which affect nontraditional community college students, those that constitute individual action not necessarily role- or rule-bound are of considerable salience to nontraditional students, especially disadvantaged students. These independent actors, whose individual agendas are often in play, are referred to as institutional squires or "street-level bureaucrats" (Lipsky, 1980). Institutional squires at various levels, from the program level of faculty and coordinators to the level of state system presidents, enact personal preferences and agendas either directly or through policy. Additionally, organizational power arrangements or configurations privilege some organizational members and influencers so that they have substantial power in the decisions and actions of organizations. Such influence may be vested within groups or individuals (Mintzberg, 1989). The president of the North Carolina community college system took the authority and advantage of his position to fulfill a personal agenda of improving higher education opportunities for Latino students, many of whom are not legal immigrants and are often stymied by institutional regulations and federal law. The chancellor of California's community college system, the largest in the nation, expressed not only a personal agenda for the state's community colleges, but also awareness of his influential position. Both critic and champion, the chancellor of the state's 109 community colleges articulated the failings and shortcomings of state policies and funding practices and focused on the lower socioeconomic strata of the state comprised of eighteen to twenty-four year olds, which is sapping the economic life out of the state. His intention was to resuscitate "the whole bottom end of that system." For him "that is a personal agenda of mine to do something about that and we have already started."

Employing what Mintzberg (1983) terms the "missionary configuration" of power, that is, aligning external and internal influencers through strongly held belief systems, the two system executives were able to exercise power for specific issues and causes. They potentially enabled large immigrant populations in North Carolina and California to move beyond their starting points of educational deficiencies to higher educational, and ultimately, economic levels. Compared with the influence of individual faculty or administrators at community colleges, these policy executives affected large populations through their actions.

Although some literature suggests that institutional effects are far outweighed by student effects (Bailey and others, 2005), this may not be the case for disadvantaged students. Large-scale interventions such as those brought about by government legislation, including state propositions to curtail services to undocumented immigrants, can have profound effects upon large numbers of students. In Arizona, public services to noncitizens and nonresidents are viewed as illegal acts. At the time of my investigation in North Carolina, undocumented immigrants could not register for credit programs at community colleges or universities (this law has since been altered, yet recently reversed to discriminate against undocumented immigrants). Yet institutional actions can also have important consequences if those actions, tacitly agreed to by institutional members, ignore system and state policies and laws that exclude or disadvantage populations from equal participation in postsecondary education. In these cases, institutional effects are unquestionably significant.

At the several colleges I observed, college employees, from presidents to midlevel administrators to faculty and staff, rely upon personal ethical standards and ignore state or federal policy so that students were not harmed. They resorted to "illegitimate" behaviors or "spin" rationales for their actions to accommodate students. They helped students to enroll in credit programs even though they were undocumented immigrants, to finance their education even though they might not qualify for grants or scholarships, and to ensure that programs and instructional attention were available even in the face of legislative and public political opposition or indifference. These actions are responses to conditions perpetuated by exogenous forces—by federal and state policy, by family economic status and domestic conditions, by previous school experiences, and by employers and agencies. Institutional efforts affect change both for individual students and for student groups: they frustrate, curtail, impede, or indeed nullify the expected trajectory of student participation and achievement based upon student characteristics.

As long as exogenous forces and influences continue to disadvantage students, institutional agents—squires—will likely continue to rescue students and aid them in educational attainment and social mobility. This is one of the central empirically observed and acclaimed characteristics of community colleges. Yet, to reach classes or categories of students—underrepresented minority populations, low-income students, undocumented immigrant students, students with disabilities, single-parent students, and academically disadvantaged students—state and federal policies and practices are among the influences that must be examined for their deleterious effects and altered when found wanting. For example, recent state proclamations, interpretations, and referenda (e.g., in North Carolina and Arizona) that either explicitly or implicitly forbid the enrollment of undocumented immigrants in community colleges have deleterious effects not only upon those who reside in their state on a personal level, but also upon the state's economy. Additionally, policies that limit state or federal aid based upon student enrollment status (fulltime vs. part-time) have little ethical justification and instead are discriminatory, particularly affecting specific student populations.

Community college practitioners cannot be held accountable for these influences, but legislators can. Legislators and other elected officials do not always understand the issues and certainly not the consequences of state and federal policies that affect community college students and potential students (Levin and Levin, 2007). The strengthening and increasing of efforts by community college leaders and their professional organizations to inform and educate elected officials may be one step. These community college leaders can be informed by understanding the effects of state and federal policies upon specific student populations within their institutions.

References

Bailey, T. R., and others. *The Effects of Institutional Factors on the Success of Community College Students.* New York: Columbia University, Teachers College, Community College Research Center, 2005.

Bowl, M. *Non-Traditional Entrants to Higher Education.* Stoke on Trent, U.K.: Trentham Books, 2003.

Clark, B. *The Open Door College: A Case Study.* New York: McGraw-Hill, 1960.

Cohen, A., and Brawer, F. *The American Community College.* San Francisco: Jossey-Bass, 2003.

Dougherty, K. *The Contradictory College.* Albany: State University of New York Press, 1994.

Frye, J. "Educational Paradigms in the Professional Literature of the Community College." In J. Smart (ed.), *Higher Education: Handbook of Theory and Research, X.* New York: Agathon Press, 1994.

Hasenfeld, Y. *Human Service Organizations.* Upper Saddle River, N.J.: Prentice Hall, 1983.

Holland, D. C., Lachicotte Jr., W., Skinner, D., and Cain, C. *Identity and Agency in Cultural Worlds.* Cambridge, Mass.: Harvard University Press, 1998.

Labaree, D. "Public Goods, Private Goods: The American Struggle over Educational Goals." *American Educational Research Journal,* 1997, 34(1), 39–81.

Levin, J., and Levin, J. S. *The Costs of Education.* Riverside: University of California, Riverside, California Community College Collaborative, 2007. Videotape.

Levin, J. S. *Non-Traditional Students and Community Colleges: The Conflict of Justice and Neo-Liberalism.* New York: Palgrave Macmillan, 2007.

Lipsky, M. *Street-Level Bureaucracy.* New York: Russell Sage Foundation, 1980.

Mintzberg, H. *Power in and Around Organizations.* Upper Saddle River, N.J.: Prentice Hall, 1983.

Mintzberg, H. *Mintzberg on Management: Inside Our Strange World of Organizations.* New York: Free Press, 1989.

Pascarella, E. T., and Terenzini, P. *How College Affects Students: A Third Decade of Research.* San Francisco: Jossey-Bass, 2005.

Rawls, J. *Political Liberalism.* New York: Columbia University Press, 1993.

Rawls, J. *A Theory of Justice.* Cambridge, Mass.: Belknap Press, 1999.

Shaw, K., Goldrick-Rab, S., Mazzeo, C., and Jacobs, J. A. "Putting Poor People to Work: How the Work-First Ideology Eroded College Access for the Poor." Unpublished paper, 2005.

Silva, T., Cahalan, M., Lacireno-Paquet, N., and Mathematica Policy Research. *Adult Education Participation Decisions and Barriers: Review of Conceptual Frameworks and Empirical Studies.* Washington, D.C.: U.S. Department of Education, Office of Educational Research and Development, National Center for Education Statistics, 1998.

Slaughter, S., and Rhoades, G. *Academic Capitalism and the New Economy: Markets, State, and Higher Education.* Baltimore, Md.: Johns Hopkins University Press, 2004.

JOHN S. LEVIN *is Bank of America Professor of Education Leadership and director of the California Community College Collaborative in the Graduate School of Education at the University of California, Riverside.*

NEW DIRECTIONS FOR COMMUNITY COLLEGES • DOI: 10.1002/cc

10

Correlating characteristics of underprepared students with undesirable outcomes is a popular but ineffective attempt to meet challenges posed by increasing student diversity and pressures for institutional accountability. This volume highlights how campus environments—the rules, practices, facilities, and climates of community colleges—might be sculpted to better foster student success.

Transmuting Resistance to Change

Pam Schuetz, Jim Barr

> However beautiful the strategy, you should occasionally look at the results.
> —Winston Churchill

Community colleges are often described as the open door to American higher education, yet for decades significant proportions of the student population have left before achieving their educational objectives. Typically, high rates of student attrition and other negative outcomes are associated with deficiencies in student precollege characteristics, involvement or commitment in classroom, and extracurricular activities (Brawer, 1996). According to this perspective, the cause of negative student outcomes is students who do not or cannot devote enough physical and psychological energy to the academic experience. Thus, attrition of underprepared students is characterized as mostly beyond the control of the college. Following Tinto's (1982) observation that national retention rates are historically stable, but that individual institutions can and do improve student outcomes, this volume sketches a broader view, acknowledging the complex joint responsibility of students and institutions for student success.

Characteristics and behaviors of students who tend to succeed are well documented, much more so than characteristics and behaviors of colleges promoting positive outcomes of underprepared students. Tinto (2005) asserts that institutions that take student success seriously would stop tinkering at the margins of institutional life and make enhancing student success the

NEW DIRECTIONS FOR COMMUNITY COLLEGES, no. 144, Winter 2008 © 2008 Wiley Periodicals, Inc.
Published online in Wiley InterScience (www.interscience.wiley.com) • DOI: 10.1002/cc.350

linchpin about which they organize their activities. They would move beyond the provision of add-on services and establish those educational conditions within the institution that promote the success of all, not just some, students. To be serious about student success, institutions would recognize that the roots of attrition lie not only in their students and the situations they face, but also in the very character of the educational settings, now assumed to be natural to higher education, in which they ask students to learn (p. 1).

As demands for institutional accountability increase and growing proportions of underprepared community college students are arriving on campus, this volume addresses the important task of identifying promising new perspectives and practices that offer colleges more effective leverage over student outcomes. Some of the perspectives and methods described in or extrapolated from chapters in this volume are included here.

Study Campus Environments

As Whisnant (1979) observes, a college campus can be seen as an educational metaphor, "a concrete expression of an educational world view; the dominant value system; the nature of knowledge itself; the processes of teaching and learning; the intellectual, physical and psychological status of [students]; and the role of the university [or community college] in society." Thus, physical, instructional, and sociocultural aspects of campus environments can be interpreted as dynamic expressions of both how learning has been enabled and constrained over the history of a particular institution and how it can be improved. In particular, campus choices that "celebrate the natural curiosity, energy, and diversity of its students as its most essential resource" provide "useful point[s] of leverage . . . for reducing tension and bringing about change."

Make the Campus Environment Read

The type and quality of student experiences in and out of the classroom communicate a college's educational philosophy to students, letting them know where they stand in the hierarchy of institutional priorities. Wenger (1998) argues that the quantity and quality of connections made in the learning environment are mediated by boundary objects (artifacts, documents, terms, and concepts) and brokering (connections made for people), which are largely under the control of campus personnel. Symbolic interactionists would point to the power of rituals and other symbolic actions, suggesting that infusing repetitive events like orientation or career development activities with elements of ritual and symbolism can strengthen their functions (Alexander, Giesen, and Mast, 2006; Cook and King, 2004).

Thus, a paucity of campus maps or signage, inadequate academic and career counseling, or chilly facilities or interpersonal climate can discourage students, especially the growing proportion of students who arrive as authentic beginners. Shugart and Romano in Chapter Three describe how to embed procedural cues and "how to learn" skills into campus environments and argues that these strategies become ever more important to support the success of these students. Difficult or confusing experiences are especially discouraging for new students who do not have specific campus expertise to fall back on and may account for a good portion of precensus departures.

Build Bridges

McGrath and Spear (1991) suggest a point of view that offers colleges more leverage over outcomes of underprepared students: "The educational problem of nontraditionality is not really primarily a problem of low skills or spotty previous high school achievement, or low income, or family responsibilities. . . . The educational challenge for community colleges is the construction of bridges of understanding across which students may move from nontraditional backgrounds to competent membership in the educated community." Several authors in this volume, including McGrath and Tobia in Chapter Four and Jaswal and Jaswal in Chapter Five, describe building "bridges of understanding" based upon both theoretical and practical understandings of the challenges and resources that campus environments pose for students.

Ask Students

Levin (2000) observes that "the history of education reform is a history of doing things to other people, supposedly for their own good. Each level in the hierarchy of education believes it knows best what those at lower levels need to do, and has little shyness about telling them or, just as often, forcing them." If we free ourselves from narrow methodological habits of targeting students as the problem in negative outcomes, more robust opportunities for innovation and improvement emerge.

To understand and eventually shape influences of campus environments on student experiences and success, we will need to know more about related campus dynamics. As Astin (1993) points out, "perhaps the richest source of data on the students' environmental experiences is the students themselves." Making use of this rich source of data by asking students about their campus experiences, as Levin does in Chapter Nine, is an important first step in understanding and sculpting institutional environments to foster student engagement and success.

Develop and Apply Community College Theory

Theory is a necessary tool if sense is to be made of the multitude of variables and dynamics that appear to influence student outcomes within and across campus environments. Until recently, community college persistence research has been limited by atheoretical or descriptive approaches or by theories about four-year institutions that embed assumptions that distort observations and findings for two-year colleges. Theory building for community colleges, such as that described by Schuetz in Chapter Two, is needed to explain why some students stay while others leave and how institutional policies, practices, facilities, climates, and resource allocation might foster or hinder student engagement. New theories based upon community college dynamics are needed to help guide positive interventions and improve performance at institutional levels.

Examine Existing Measures

Some of our most familiar measures of student success are flawed. For example, persistence rates are typically calculated as the ratio of students who return in fall term after having enrolled as first-time fulltime students in the fall of the previous year. This familiar measure both overstates and understates persistence figures.

Fall-to-fall persistence rates ignore up to an estimated additional 25 percent of students who leave campus before the first official enrollment census is conducted in the second, third, or fourth week of the term. These rates also focus on students enrolled for the first time anywhere in higher education, whereas colleges also admit significant proportions of students who are first-time attendees at a particular institution but have transferred from another institution or re-entered higher education after a long absence. Each of these groups may have different fall-to-fall persistence rates than true beginners. In addition, fall-to-fall persistence rates blind us to lower spring-to-spring persistence rates. At one community college, for example, fall-to-fall rates averaged close to 50 percent over the last ten years; spring-to-spring rates averaged 33 percent over the same period. Furthermore, one-year persistence rates may also conceal a significant number of students who are on probation, technically still enrolled at the one-year mark but making minimal progress before being dismissed or dropping out shortly thereafter. This is only one example of the shortcomings embedded in familiar measures of student success. Many more exist such as those examined by Goble, Rosenbaum, and Stephan in Chapter Six.

Identify Key Effectiveness Measures

Although persistence as it is currently evaluated does not provide a realistic representation of student behavior, it is still one of the most sensitive measures of how a college is doing overall. For example, when persistence rates do not improve, neither does anything else. When a higher proportion of students continues to attend, there is a proportionally higher probability of successful progress in other courses and in conventional outcomes such as the number of degrees, certificates, and transfers to four-year institutions.

Two other equally sensitive measures are success in English writing and in math sequence courses. In 2009, California community colleges will require that students successfully complete higher-level math and English writing courses than in the past. For these colleges, the most telling indicators will be any shifts in the success of courses that are one level below transfer-level English writing and two levels below transfer-level math. Although students will be required to enroll in and successfully pass the next higher-level course to meet the new graduation requirements, both of these lower-level courses have historically had notoriously low success rates. Any positive change for student success at this "underprepared" level, as with increases in persistence, would be a clear indication of improvement that will impact the entire college. Illowsky in Chapter Eight describes the development and implementation of an emerging basic skills initiative.

Redesign Inequitable Campus Policies

Some policies and practices favor one population of students more than others. For example, priority enrollment and course shopping policies tend to favor experienced students and students in special support programs over beginning student populations because the former are typically allowed early enrollment in classes. Early registrants may engage in course shopping: registering for more courses than they intend to take, attending the first session or two, and then dropping those they do not like. Meanwhile, beginning students may find they cannot enroll in any of the classes they were hoping to take even though several weeks into the term these same classes may be underenrolled once course shoppers drop out. Policies regarding priority enrollment and course shopping should be redesigned to provide more equitable distribution of opportunities to the student population as a whole. For example, rolling priorities over time could provide incentives and opportunities for all students to finish programs faster.

Similarly, student participants involved in boutique or add-on programs such as learning communities, bridge programs, single-parent support groups, counseling or human development courses, and general education diploma (GED) programs typically report feeling well supported in their transition to college. However, strategies and practices of these small resource-intensive programs, such as increased counseling, tutoring, and financial support, cannot be extended to the entire population in their current forms under present funding realities. Differential achievement based on inequities in such distribution of campus resources may reinforce the idea that the student is the problem. Of course, the intriguing thing about all support programs is that from one perspective they have served as laboratories to educate us about key elements that have the potential to be integrated into the classroom and campus at large.

Any effort to institutionalize the key elements of these practices can start with an inquiry to determine which common elements are found throughout all support programs: for example, time-management practices, self-efficacy issues associated with underpreparedness, and basic how-to-learn techniques associated with all learning. Although some support programs such as learning communities stress student engagement in paired courses, it is not difficult to imagine that any classroom or campus environment can be a learning community when instructors break from the traditions of lecture to create learning environments that spark student interest and engagement in and out of class. Examples of redesigning campus policies to serve the general student population occur throughout this volume, but especially in Chapters Three through Six.

Take Notice of Early Departures

Very little attention is paid to students who leave during the first few weeks of the term. Bers and Nyden (2000–2001) point out that students who leave before the first official enrollment census is taken in the second, third, or fourth week of the term are not included in enrollment summaries or considered to have enrolled at all, rendering them virtually invisible to the institution. This significant blind spot should be eliminated. Every student is valuable and research into the dynamics of early attrition may provide insights that will help address longer-term disengagement and attrition as well.

Encourage Early Engagement

The first days and weeks of the college experience are foundational: expectations meet campus realities, attitudes fostering or hindering academic success are reinforced or newly created, and choices are made about whether and how to engage in the college experience. Students are more open to change when they first arrive on campus, yet most institutions squander this fleeting opportunity to truly engage beginning students.

For example, colleges could redevelop orientation activities and devote the first several weeks of each term to give students an overview of how the campus works, show what kinds of educational opportunities are related to what sorts of academic and career options, and teach students how to find out more to make best use of those opportunities as time goes on (Kuh, 1999; Levitz and Noel, 1989; Lewallen, 1993). Shugart and Romano's recommendation in Chapter Three to identify the top twenty most difficult courses that first-time students enroll in creates a clear target to focus efforts that could better support students at the front door. Both basic skills math and English writing courses that would fall in this top twenty list are characterized by large enrollments and historically low success rates.

Basic skills composition courses could foster student engagement and reflection by including assignments that explore how to identify educational objectives or that ask students to write letters to their younger selves or to first-time students about lessons learned since starting college. Use of

English writing courses to address issues associated with underprepared-ness and lack of sophistication with college practices could be a very novel approach to addressing the needs of these students. Similarly, finding more ways to introduce students to the academic and employment opportunities associated with different programs of study, perhaps through rotating departmental job fairs staffed by faculty and advanced students, could fos-ter engagement and outcomes by stimulating students' goal-setting and seeking behaviors (Schuetz, Chapter Two).

Cultivate Systematic Peer Support

Given the relative sizes and characteristics of student populations compared to other institutional resources, the student population itself may be the only campus resource large enough to meet the ongoing needs of beginning stu-dents for positive contact and role modeling. Happily, "in the aggregate, inter-action with peers is probably the most pervasive and powerful force in student persistence and degree completion. The recent research suggests one dynamic at work is students' attraction to other students who are like themselves in various ways, including attitudes and values, and a second powerful influence is students' socialization to peer group norms through progressive conformity, which encourages students to adapt their goals and values to accommodate those of the peer group." Collaborative learning formats include peer men-toring, "first-year seminars, supplemental instruction, academic advising, summer bridge programs, undergraduate research programs, living-learning centers, and learning communities" (Pascarella and Terenzini, 2005).

Peer support can be simple yet pervasive. For example, one campus simply recruited experienced students to wear red support bracelets so that new students could see whom to ask for basic information. New students who might feel intimidated by teachers and counselors are more likely to ask basic questions of an informed fellow student. Student help chat rooms, student-staffed telephone help lines, supplemental instruction, peer tutor-ing, and in-person student-staffed mentoring stations around campus could provide ramps for incoming students who perceive a wall of confusing choices, bureaucratic obstacles, and academic challenges. Tiered mentoring systems, as described by Jaswal and Jaswal in Chapter Five, represent more structured ways to capture veteran student expertise to help anchor new students more effectively on campus.

Of course, students would have to be trained, supervised, and paid to carry out tiered mentoring and most other support services. Nonetheless finding funding for students through avenues such as the federal work-study program is more feasible than hiring more counselors and other staff. Furthermore, employing students as mentors on campus not only helps mentors financially, but increases the probability of beneficial interactions with peers and faculty as they work to expand their own knowledge of opportunities offered on campus. Indeed, many collaborative experiences tend to benefit both students giving and the students receiving help—a win-win situation.

Transmute Resistance to Change

Community colleges, like most other educational institutions and systems, are organized around top-down hierarchies of power and control, casting students as relatively passive recipients of education rather than active participants. It is likely that both conscious and unconscious resistance from a broad range of constituencies will be encountered when shifting toward a more engaged and collaborative perspective on learning.

Conscious resistance to positive change on community college campuses might be transmuted by drawing constituencies into mutually beneficial partnerships developed to meet individual and institutional needs. Unconscious resistance to effective research and practice is more difficult to work with because it typically arises from rarely challenged habits of thought. For example, as community college policy makers, researchers, and practitioners, we have had many years of personal successes in four-year educational arenas. Therefore, the lens through which we habitually look to design and implement interventions to improve the success of underprepared students is likely to be that of a successful student familiar with the dynamics of four-year campus environments. This perspective has significant shortcomings for research and practice related to underprepared community college students. As K. Patricia Cross (1971) observed with the expansion of nontraditional student enrollment during the 1960s, "Access to education that is inappropriate for the development of individual talents may represent nothing more than prolonged captivity in an environment that offers little more than an opportunity to repeat the damaging experiences with school failure that New Students know so well." Ironically, then, both our greatest challenge and greatest hope in fostering access and success of underprepared students may be to let go of what we know and practice redefining problems from community college students' perspectives.

For example, Rendon (1994) asserts that when underrepresented "students who came to college expecting to fail suddenly began to believe in their innate capacity to learn and to become successful college students," the key factor was not student involvement, as is often emphasized in studies framed by Tinto's (1975) four-year theory of departure, but incidents "where some individual, either in- or out-of-class, took an active interest in them—when someone took the initiative to lend a helping hand, to do something that affirmed them . . . supported them in their academic endeavors and social adjustment." This observation aligns with Van Buskirk and McGrath's (1999) assertion that effective campus environments must first support the current identities of organizational members rather than trying to foist a new, even if "good," identity upon them. By offering a space for the student to feel comfortable as he is now and also putting in place "symbols, structures and practices. . . that spur creativity and growth," community colleges can foster engagement of underprepared students and generate interpersonal growth among students, faculty, and staff.

Conclusion

Underprepared students have been a significant presence in community colleges for decades. The growing size of this student population and the urgent reality of workforce accountability and other demands that did not exist forty years ago are pushing colleges to find more effective ways to support success for such students. This volume steps outside entrenched habits of viewing the underprepared student as the central problem in improving student outcomes to highlight new questions and approaches that include seeing campus challenges from students' perspectives.

We have a very elegant educational framework developed, and community colleges certainly have the willingness, ability, and creativity to serve underprepared students more effectively; we just do not know quite how to do so yet. However, there is a huge amount of fertile ground to be plowed, ripe with potential and opportunity for colleges and students. If community college policy makers, researchers, and practitioners can find the courage and willingness to appreciate the fact that they are as underprepared for their underprepared students as these students are for college-level curriculum, it could signal the beginning of a major paradigm shift and a new universe of possibilities opening for exploration by both community colleges and their students. This volume describes perspectives and methods that can help community colleges move into an ideal position to catapult engagement and achievement to the next level.

References

Alexander, J. C., Giesen, B., and Mast, J. L. (eds.). *Social Performance: Symbolic Action, Cultural Pragmatics, and Ritual.* Cambridge: Cambridge University Press, 2006.

Astin, A. *Assessment for Excellence.* Phoenix, Ariz.: Oryx Press, 1993.

Bers, T. H., and Nyden, G. "The Disappearing Student: Students Who Leave Before the Census Date." *Journal of College Student Retention: Research, Theory and Practice,* 2000–2001, 2(3), 205–217.

Brawer, F. B. "Retention-Attrition in the Nineties." *ERIC Digest.* Los Angeles: ERIC Clearinghouse for Community Colleges, 1996.

Cook, B., and King, J. *Low-Income Adults in Profile: Improving Lives through Higher Education.* Washington, D.C.: American Council on Education, 2004.

Cross, K. P. *Beyond the Open Door: New Students to Higher Education.* San Francisco: Jossey-Bass, 1971.

Kuh, G. D. "How Are We Doing? Tracking the Quality of the Undergraduate Experience, 1960s to the Present." *Review of Higher Education,* 1999, 22(2), 99–120.

Levin, B. "Putting Students at the Centre of Educational Reform." *Journal of Educational Change,* 2000, 1(2), 155–172.

Levitz, R., and Noel, L. "Connecting Students to Institutions: Keys to Retention and Success." In M. Upcraft, J. Gardner, and Associates (eds.), *The Freshman Year Experience: Helping Students to Survive and Succeed in College.* San Francisco: Jossey-Bass, 1989.

Lewallen, W. C. "The Impact of Being 'Undecided' on College-Student Persistence." *Journal of College Student Development,* 1993, *34*(2), 103–112.

McGrath, D., and Spear, M. B. *The Academic Crisis of the Community College.* Albany: State University of New York Press, 1991.

Pascarella, E. T., and Terenzini, P. T. *How College Affects Students: A Third Decade of Research.* San Francisco: Jossey-Bass, 2005.

Rendon, L. I. "Validating Culturally Diverse Students: Toward a New Model of Learning and Student Development." *Innovative Higher Education,* 1994, *19*(1), 33–51.

Tinto, V. "Dropouts from Higher Education: A Theoretical Synthesis of the Recent Literature." *Review of Educational Research,* 1975, *45,* 89–125.

Tinto, V. "Limits of Theory and Practice in Student Attrition." *Journal of Higher Education,* 1982, *53*(6), 687–700.

Tinto, V. "Taking Student Success Seriously: Rethinking the First Year of College." Paper presented at the Ninth Annual Intersession Academic Affairs Forum, California State University, Fullerton, Jan. 26, 2005. Accessed Aug. 30, 2008, at http://fdc.fullerton.edu/events/05–01/acadforum/Taking%20Success%20Seriously.pdf.

Van Buskirk, W., and McGrath, D. "Organizational Cultures as Holding Environments: A Psychodynamic Look at Organizational Symbolism." *Human Relations,* 1999, *52*(6), 805–832.

Wenger, E. *Communities of Practice: Learning, Meaning, and Identity.* Cambridge: Cambridge University Press, 1998.

Whisnant, D. E. "The University as a Space and the Future of the University." *Journal of Higher Education,* 1979, *50*(4), 544–558.

PAM SCHUETZ *is a postdoctoral fellow at Northwestern University in Evanston, Illinois.*

JIM BARR *is a senior research analyst at American River College in Sacramento, California.*

NEW DIRECTIONS FOR COMMUNITY COLLEGES • DOI: 10.1002/cc

INDEX

Statement of Ownership, Management, and Circulation
(All Periodicals Publications Except Requester Publications)

1. Publication Title	2. Publication Number	3. Filing Date
New Directions for Community Colleges	0 1 9 4 _ 3 0 8 1	10/1/2008

4. Issue Frequency	5. Number of Issues Published Annually	6. Annual Subscription Price
Quarterly	4	$209

7. Complete Mailing Address of Known Office of Publication (Not printer) (Street, city, county, state, and ZIP+4®)

Wiley Subscriptions Services, Inc. at Jossey-Bass, 989 Market St., San Francisco, CA 94103

Contact Person: Joe Schuman

Telephone (Include area code): 415-782-3232

8. Complete Mailing Address of Headquarters or General Business Office of Publisher (Not printer)

Wiley Subscriptions Services, Inc., 111 River Street, Hoboken, NJ 07030

9. Full Names and Complete Mailing Addresses of Publisher, Editor, and Managing Editor (Do not leave blank)

Publisher (Name and complete mailing address)

Wiley Subscriptions Services, Inc., A Wiley Company at San Francisco, 989 Market St., San Francisco, CA 94103-1741

Editor (Name and complete mailing address)

Arthur M. Cohen, Eric Clearinghouse for Community Colleges, 3051 Moore Hall, Box 95121, Los Angeles, CA 90095

Managing Editor (Name and complete mailing address)

None

10. Owner (Do not leave blank. If the publication is owned by a corporation, give the name and address of the corporation immediately followed by the names and addresses of all stockholders owning or holding 1 percent or more of the total amount of stock. If not owned by a corporation, give the names and addresses of the individual owners. If owned by a partnership or other unincorporated firm, give its name and address as well as those of each individual owner. If the publication is published by a nonprofit organization, give its name and address.)

Full Name	Complete Mailing Address
Wiley Subscriptions Services	111 River Street, Hoboken, NJ
(see attached list)	

11. Known Bondholders, Mortgagees, and Other Security Holders Owning or Holding 1 Percent or More of Total Amount of Bonds, Mortgages, or Other Securities. If none, check box ☑ None

Full Name	Complete Mailing Address

12. Tax Status (For completion by nonprofit organizations authorized to mail at nonprofit rates) (Check one)

The purpose, function, and nonprofit status of this organization and the exempt status for federal income tax purposes:

☐ Has Not Changed During Preceding 12 Months
☐ Has Changed During Preceding 12 Months (Publisher must submit explanation of change with this statement)

13. Publication Title	14. Issue Date for Circulation Data
New Directions for Community Colleges	Summer 2008

15. Extent and Nature of Circulation		Average No. Copies Each Issue During Preceding 12 Months	No. Copies of Single Issue Published Nearest to Filing Date
a. Total Number of Copies (Net press run)		1535	1456
b. Paid Circulation (By Mail and Outside the Mail)	(1) Mailed Outside-County Paid Subscriptions Stated on PS Form 3541 (Include paid distribution above nominal rate, advertiser's proof copies, and exchange copies)	644	625
	(2) Mailed In-County Paid Subscriptions Stated on PS Form 3541 (Include paid distribution above nominal rate, advertiser's proof copies, and exchange copies)	0	0
	(3) Paid Distribution Outside the Mails Including Sales Through Dealers and Carriers, Street Vendors, Counter Sales, and Other Paid Distribution Outside USPS®	0	0
	(4) Paid Distribution by Other Classes of Mail Through the USPS (e.g. First-Class Mail®)		0
c. Total Paid Distribution (Sum of 15b (1), (2),(3), and (4))		644	625
d. Free or Nominal Rate Distribution (By Mail and Outside the Mail)	(1) Free or Nominal Rate Outside-County Copies Included on PS Form 3541	132	129
	(2) Free or Nominal Rate In-County Copies Included on PS Form 3541	0	0
	(3) Free or Nominal Rate Copies Mailed at Other Classes Through the USPS (e.g. First-Class Mail)	0	0
	(4) Free or Nominal Rate Distribution Outside the Mail (Carriers or other means)	0	0
e. Total Free or Nominal Rate Distribution (Sum of 15d (1), (2), (3) and (4)		132	129
f. Total Distribution (Sum of 15c and 15e)	▶	776	754
g. Copies not Distributed (See Instructions to Publishers #4 (page #3))	▶	759	702
h. Total (Sum of 15f and g)	▶	1535	1456
i. Percent Paid (15c divided by 15f times 100)	▶	83%	83%

16. Publication of Statement of Ownership

☐ If the publication is a general publication, publication of this statement is required. Will be printed in the Winter 2008 issue of this publication.

☐ Publication not required.

17. Signature and Title of Editor, Publisher, Business Manager, or Owner

Susan E. Lewis, VP & Publisher - Periodicals   *Susan Lewis*

Date: 10/1/2008

I certify that all information furnished on this form is true and complete. I understand that anyone who furnishes false or misleading information on this form or who omits material or information requested on the form may be subject to criminal sanctions (including fines and imprisonment) and/or civil sanctions (including civil penalties).

NEW DIRECTIONS FOR COMMUNITY COLLEGE

ORDER FORM SUBSCRIPTION AND SINGLE ISSUES

DISCOUNTED BACK ISSUES:

Use this form to receive 20% off all back issues of *New Directions for Community College*.
All single issues priced at **$23.20** (normally $29.00)

TITLE	ISSUE NO.	ISBN

Call 888-378-2537 or see mailing instructions below. When calling, mention the promotional code JB9ND to receive your discount. For a complete list of issues, please visit www.josseybass.com/go/ndcc

SUBSCRIPTIONS: (1 YEAR, 4 ISSUES)

☐ New Order ☐ Renewal

U.S.	☐ Individual: $89	☐ Institutional: $228
CANADA/MEXICO	☐ Individual: $89	☐ Institutional: $268
ALL OTHERS	☐ Individual: $113	☐ Institutional: $302

Call 888-378-2537 or see mailing and pricing instructions below.
Online subscriptions are available at www.interscience.wiley.com

ORDER TOTALS:

Issue / Subscription Amount: $ _____

Shipping Amount: $ _____
(for single issues only – subscription prices include shipping)

Total Amount: $ _____

SHIPPING CHARGES:

First Item	$5.00
Each Add'l Item	$3.00

(No sales tax for U.S. subscriptions. Canadian residents, add GST for subscription orders. Individual rate subscriptions must be paid by personal check or credit card. Individual rate subscriptions may not be resold as library copies.)

BILLING & SHIPPING INFORMATION:

☐ **PAYMENT ENCLOSED:** *(U.S. check or money order only. All payments must be in U.S. dollars.)*

☐ **CREDIT CARD:** ☐ VISA ☐ MC ☐ AMEX

Card number _____ Exp. Date _____

Card Holder Name_____ Card Issue # _____

Signature _____ Day Phone _____

☐ **BILL ME:** *(U.S. institutional orders only. Purchase order required.)*

Purchase order # _____
Federal Tax ID 13559302 • GST 89102-8052

Name_____

Address_____

Phone_____ E-mail_____

Copy or detach page and send to: **John Wiley & Sons, PTSC, 5th Floor**
989 Market Street, San Francisco, CA 94103-1741

Order Form can also be faxed to: **888-481-2665**

PROMO JB9ND